Criminal Justice
Recent Scholarship

Edited by
Marilyn McShane and Frank P. Williams III

A Series from LFB Scholarly

A Zero-Tolerance Juvenile Alcohol Law

Why Legislation Won't Work

John A. Lewis

LFB Scholarly Publishing LLC
El Paso 2009

Library of Congress Cataloging-in-Publication Data

Lewis, John A. (John Allen), 1957-
A zero-tolerance juvenile alcohol law : why legislation won't work / John
A. Lewis.
p. cm. -- (Criminal justice : recent scholarship)
Includes bibliographical references and index.
ISBN 978-1-59332-367-7 (alk. paper)
1. Teenagers--Alcohol use. 2. Drunk driving--Prevention. I. Title.
HV5135.L483 2009
345.73'0247--dc22
2009018623

ISBN 978-1-59332-367-7

Printed on acid-free 250-year-life paper.

Manufactured in the United States of America.

Table of Contents

TABLES

FIGURES

Preface

Currently, there is a dilemma about how to handle alcohol related offensives, especially those that result in Driving While Intoxicated (DWI). The National Highway Transportation Safety Administration (NHTSA) reports that there are approximately 1.5 million DWI arrests each year, with approximately 500,000 being repeat offenders. Additionally, based on information provided by 23 states, the NHTSA estimates that 1,156,672 individuals have been convicted three or more times for DWI, and of these approximately 111,000 have five or more convictions.

A common policy reaction, based on deterrence theory, is to increase the severity of sanctions for those caught offending and to increase the certainty that those who offend will be convicted. There are several problems with this approach. First, can our jails and prisons accommodate the volume of traffic an incarceration approach would generate? Secondly, as sanctions become more severe, do we as a society risk causing more harm than good?

Envision an irrational drunk driver behind the wheel of an automobile who already has two or more DWI convictions, knowing an additional conviction would get him a minimum three year prison sentence. What is the offender's initial reaction when the police attempt to stop the vehicle? If the offender eludes the police the offender risks one year possible for reckless driving and another for evading the police if they get a license plate number and can place him as the operator of the vehicle. A DWI charge is not available since the offender was not caught intoxicated behind the wheel of the vehicle. Is running worth the risk? Are the chances of flight increased if the police department has a "no continued pursuit" policy? Draconian policies could result in more harm than good.

Another issue is that as more laws are passed to deter alcohol use, net widening will occur and more people, especially juveniles, will be entered into the criminal justice system. For example, in some states juveniles are cited for transporting alcohol, even though the adult who purchased the alcohol is in the vehicle. The concept behind the law is to prevent juvenile access to alcohol, but the law as written can ensnare those who had no intent of violating the law. The law is punishing juveniles for what might happen, instead of focusing on what did happen. Additionally, the law often is not related to the presence of alcohol, but to who is operating the vehicle; if it is the juvenile an offense has occurred, if it is the adult, no offense has occurred, the alcohol has become irrelevant.

There is little disagreement about the seriousness of DWI offenses. The disagreement is about policy, with the current approach favoring retribution and incarceration, instead of deterrence and rehabilitation. The argument made in this book is that a retribution and incarceration approach has little chance of success and will only add to the problem through higher incarceration rates, the threat of more severe offending, and the implementation of additional policies that will cause net widening.

ACKNOWLEDGEMENTS:
My deep appreciation to those who provided data (NHTSA FARS, OH and PA Departments of Transportation, OH and PA state police); my colleagues for their support and editing; and my wife Malia and daughter Melinda for their support, love, and forgiving my absences from the family.

Chapter 1

DUI Laws: Risk Reduction or Risk Enhancement

In an attempt to reduce fatality traffic accidents involving intoxicated juveniles, lawmakers and special interest groups have attempted to legislate the issue away. Legislatures and special interest groups are clinging to the classical assumption that the threat of certain, severe, and swift punishment can "prevent disturbances and disorder amid the infinite and utterly conflicting attractions of pleasure and pain" (Beccaria, 1764/1986, p. 74). However, despite the threat of severe legal sanctions, alcohol use remains a common occurrence in adolescent youths who are seeking adult status (Arnett, 2000; Moffitt, 1993; Williams & McShane, 2004). Additionally, it is plausible that regardless of the amount of legislation passed and the severity of the penalties attached for drunk driving, the goal of ridding the roads of drunk drivers for good is one that is unachievable. Attempting to attain this goal through legislative means actually could cause more harm than good by not only creating crime, but also by increasing the risk to society as drunk drivers attempt to avoid the severe penalties associated with drunk driving .

Beccaria identified that if the punishment for a particular crime was not proportional to the harm done to society, the threat of the punishment could cause an individual to commit additional crimes in an attempt to avoid the severe punishments associated with the original offense (marginal deterrence). Criminal justice research indicates that as punishments become more certain and severe, the arrests become more difficult. Research about three strikes laws indicates that violators are more likely to risk their lives and the lives of others to avoid the third strike (Johnson & Saint-Germain, 2005). Rape was dropped from the capital punishment list, since the perpetrator had little incentive to leave the victim alive when the same punishment was plausible for both rape and homicide. Similarly, as impaired driving and underage drinking legislation becomes more punitive, violators will be more likely to risk injury to themselves and others in an attempt to avoid prosecution.

Research indicates that legislating lower Blood Alcohol Concentration (BAC) limits for juveniles does little to prevent juvenile alcohol consumption, and the associated drinking and driving (e.g., Hilton, 1984; Levy, 2002; Pogarsky, 2002; Shope & Bingham, 2002). Further, zero-tolerance juvenile alcohol policies may increase juvenile drunk driving arrest rates, while having little or no impact on juvenile alcohol related fatality accident rates. Beccaria (1764/1986) observed that "to prohibit a host of harmless acts is not to prevent the crimes to which they might lead; it is, rather, to create new crimes" (p. 74). By defining drunk driving for juveniles as the operation of a motor vehicle with a BAC level of .02 mg/ml for those under the age of 21 years old, lawmakers are attempting to prevent, or at least reduce, alcohol related juvenile fatality accidents through the use of zero-tolerance alcohol use policies.

The validity of this zero-tolerance approach to fatality accident reduction depends primarily on two variables, 1) the impact of the law on juvenile drunk driving arrest rates and 2) the impact of the law on alcohol related juvenile fatality motor vehicle accident rates.

The *2001 National Survey of Drinking and Driving* (Levy, 2002) reported that the number of juveniles who admitted (in surveys conducted bi-annually since 1995) to driving a vehicle within two hours of consuming alcohol has remained relatively stable, at 5%. Based on these responses, the passage of zero-tolerance juvenile drinking and driving legislation has failed to deter them from drinking and driving. Since the passage of the zero-tolerance juvenile drinking and driving legislation in 1996, the national rate of alcohol related juvenile fatality accidents has increased slightly each year, adding support to Levy's findings that the zero-tolerance legislation is a questionable remedy to the problem of juvenile drinking and driving.

Arguably, in restricting juveniles from consuming alcohol, legislatures and special interest groups are attempting to define virtues and vices (Hingson, 1993; Jacobs, 1989). Beccaria (1764/1986) cautioned about the ineffectiveness of legal sanctions when laws were formed by moral crusaders (interactionist perspective) and not by public accord (consensus perspective). Federal mandates have been the primary source for most state-imposed sanctions for underage drinking and juvenile drinking and driving. The Federal Uniform Drinking Age Act of 1984 (P. L. 98-363, Section 6, July 1984) failed to deter juveniles from drinking underage; thus, new directives (NHTSA 77-

96, DTD: Oct 21, 1996) were introduced to address the crime of drinking and driving by juveniles.

The essential question still remains, has establishing the juvenile drunk driving BAC level at .02 significantly changed juvenile drinking and driving behaviors? More specifically, has the Pennsylvania zero-tolerance juvenile drinking and driving legislation significantly lowered juvenile arrest rates for drunk driving (willful compliance) and/or lowered juvenile alcohol related fatality rates? Through the use of quantitative and qualitative research methods, this study evaluated the effects (deterrent and otherwise) of Pennsylvania's zero-tolerance juvenile drinking and driving laws.

Federal Mandates and Legislation Creating Crime

"The deterrence doctrine remains the philosophical foundation for modern Western criminal law and criminal justice systems" (Akers, 2000, p. 17). The primary concept underlying the deterrence doctrine is that of punishment and pleasure (Beccaria, 1764/1986; Paternoster & Bachman, 2001). If caught violating a law, the punishment must be certain, proportionately severe, and swift. For deterrence to be effective, a would-be offender must perceive all the pleasures incurred by committing an offense as being negated by the perceived punishment. Though it has formed the foundation of our punitive model of justice for over 200 years, the effectiveness of the deterrence doctrine to reduce crime has been highly debated (Akers, 2000; Saltzman, Paternoster, Waldo, & Chiricos, 1982; Scheider, 2001). Research has found limited support for deterrence hypotheses (Corbett & Simon, 1992; Erickson, Gibbs, & Jensen, 1977; Paternoster, 1987; Piquero & Rengert, 1999; Yu & Liska,

1993), especially when used in an attempt to control juveniles who consume alcohol (Evans, Neville, & Graham, 1991; Exum, 2002; Hingson & Winter, 2003; Lanza-Kaduce, 1988; Pogarsky, 2002).

In applying the deterrence doctrine, policymakers often fail to predict policy effectiveness; they either simply assume an impact based on the tenets of rational choice and/or are satisfied to appear tough on crime through punitive, deterrent-based policies. Legislation and policies often are passed with little or no idea of the true scope and severity of the problem, and with no clear measures identified to evaluate the effectiveness of the policy or legislation (Dunn, 1994).

Akers (2000) notes, "The most common policy reaction to crime problems is to call for increased penalties, more severe sentences, additions to the police force so more arrests can be made, and the increased certainty of conviction and sentencing" (p. 18). This "common policy reaction" has been the approach favored by the federal government and special interest groups in an attempt to reduce juvenile traffic accident fatalities attributed to juvenile alcohol use and drinking and driving.

Federal Mandates

The ratification of the 21st Amendment to the U.S. Constitution (1933) repealed the 18th Amendment (Prohibition). Through the 21st Amendment, States have been exclusively empowered to establish laws governing and regulating the sale, distribution, possession, and consumption of alcoholic beverages within their territorial jurisdiction (Maier, 1998). Although the federal government cannot directly mandate legislation to the states about alcohol related policies, the federal government can, and does, influence policy by placing restrictions on eligibility for federal funding.

Numerous federal initiatives have resulted in state laws being passed in an attempt to curtail both underage drinking and underage drinking and driving (those under the age of 21 years). In 1984, the National Highway Transportation Safety Administration (NHTSA) directed that to be eligible for federal highway funding, each of the states had to increase their minimum drinking age to twenty-one years of age (Lord, 2000).

The Federal Uniform Drinking Age Act of 1984 (P. L. 98-363, Section 6, July 1984) was one of the first attempts by the federal government to direct alcohol legislation to the states in an effort to reduce the number of juveniles who drink and drive (Figlio, 1995). The act directed that states raise their minimum drinking age to 21 years of age, or risk the loss of federal highway construction funds. To secure the funds, all 50 states eventually complied with the act and increased their legal drinking ages to 21. The Federal Uniform Drinking Age Act of 1984 did not require the states to modify the blood alcohol level for which the drunk driving standard was set. For Pennsylvania, and a majority of the other states, the blood alcohol level established for drunk driving was .10 mg/ml for both juveniles and adults (Hedlund, Ulmer, & Preusser, 2001).

Pennsylvania Legislation

In 1996, the federal government modified the requirements set forth in the Federal Uniform Drinking Age Act of 1984, in regards to the blood alcohol level necessary to charge a juvenile with drunk driving. The National Highway Transportation Safety Administration (NHTSA) mandated that to remain eligible for federal highway funds, all states had to enact zero-tolerance laws to combat juvenile drunk driving (NHTSA 77-96, DTD: Oct. 21, 1996). To comply with the mandate, states had to establish juvenile drunk driving blood alcohol levels at .02 mg/ml or lower. On July 2, 1996, Pennsylvania's Governor signed House Bill 2360, which contained Pennsylvania Statute 75 Pa. C. S. 3718, "Minor prohibited from operating with any alcohol in system" (Sen. M. J. White, personal communication, October 27, 2003). This "zero-tolerance" statute brought Pennsylvania into compliance with the second NHTSA directive.

Purpose of the Study

Research Intent

The intent of this research was to assess the effectiveness of Pennsylvania's zero-tolerance alcohol law in deterring juveniles from drinking and driving. The law was implemented to deter juveniles, who for the purpose of this legislation the state has defined as those under the age of 21, from operating a motor vehicle after having consumed *any* alcohol.

The effectiveness of this law, or its ability to deter offenders, was assessed using both quantitative (interrupted time-series) and qualitative (semi-structured, informal interviews and archival research) research methods. The merger of these two research paradigms produced a more accurate portrayal of the effects of Pennsylvania's zero-tolerance alcohol law, while controlling for various threats to validity.

Research Concepts

This research differed in three important aspects from most of the previous research about the impact of juvenile driving while intoxicated laws. First, it is argued that for this law to be deemed effective, it must deter would-be offenders from committing the offense of driving while intoxicated, and not just create a new crime. Previous research on the effects of drunk driving legislation has used reductions in fatality traffic accidents as a proxy measure for the effectiveness of new drinking and driving legislation, failing to account for the pre- and post-intervention drunk driving arrest rates for juveniles (Figlio, 1995; Hilton, 1984; Hingson et al., 1987; Muller, 1989; Ross, McCleary, & Epperlein, 1981; West, Hepworth, McCall, & Reich, 1989).

The argument made here is that the primary intention of the zero-tolerance juvenile drinking and driving law is behavior modification. Theoretically, an increase in the perceived severity of sanctions for drinking and driving should deter juveniles from committing this offense. If the monthly juvenile drunk driving arrest rates and juvenile alcohol related fatality vehicle accident rates are insignificantly different than the counterfactual, an increase in only the severity of legal sanctions would appear ineffective as a mean for behavior modification.

If the punishment set forth by the law is deemed as a deterrent, it would be hypothesized that juvenile driving while intoxicated arrest rates would increase immediately after the law's implementation date, and then gradually decline below, and remain below, pre-intervention rates. The initial projection of increased arrest rates is based on the lower standards set forth in the law (.10 mg/ml dropped to .02 mg/ml) to charge a juvenile with driving while intoxicated, and the initial lack of specific knowledge juveniles would possess about the law (e.g., certainty of the law's enforcement and getting caught, and the severity of punishment). However, if the law significantly and continuously increases juvenile driving while intoxicated arrest rates, based on the basic definition of deterrence and from the conceptualization employed in this project, the law has failed to deter would-be offenders and has merely increased the rate of crime by lowering the standard necessary to be considered an offender.

Second, instead of using only traffic accident fatalities as the dependent variable (e.g., Hilton, 1984; Hingson et al., 1987; Muller, 1989; Ross et al., 1981; West et al., 1989), monthly arrest rates for driving under the influence also were used as a dependent variable. The law is intended to deter juveniles from committing the offense of driving while intoxicated, thus it is necessary to identify how the law impacted the monthly drunk driving arrest rates for juveniles. Evaluating multiple measures of both adult and juvenile drunk driving arrest rates and juvenile non-alcohol and alcohol related fatality accident rates appeared to be a stronger and more complete proxy measure of the law's full impact.

Using fatality statistics as the only dependent variable fails to accurately capture the deterrent effect intended by the law. It is posited that fatality accident rates fail to capture those juveniles who are not overtly impaired, but remain in violation of the zero-tolerance law. In 2002, only 5% of all fatal traffic accidents, which occurred in Pennsylvania, involved a driver or pedestrian who had a blood alcohol level between .01 mg/ml - .07 mg/ml. Thirty-five percent of the fatality accidents involved a driver or pedestrian with a blood alcohol level of .08 mg/ml or higher, and 60% of all fatality accidents in Pennsylvania had no alcohol involvement (NHTSA, 2003). Further, it has been argued that the use of fatality traffic accidents fails to account for new automobile safety features and improvements in emergency medical on-site equipment and emergency medical response times, all of which would impact the rate of fatality accidents (Hingson, 1993).

The use of monthly rates of arrest for driving while intoxicated, while not a perfect measure, more accurately reflected the role of law enforcement in relation to the certainty of getting caught for lower levels of alcohol use. The collection and comparison of data on both juvenile arrest rates for driving while intoxicated and juvenile fatality accident rates involving alcohol added further insight into the effects of the zero-tolerance law than would have been obtained if the research had been restricted to only one outcome measure.

Finally, previous research on the effects of new juvenile-related alcohol legislation (e.g., Figlio, 1995; Hilton, 1984; Hingson et al., 1987; Muller, 1989; Ross et al., 1981; West et al., 1989) placed little emphasis on law enforcement and media effects, since these variables perceivably have little impact on fatality traffic accident rates. Since this research used monthly juvenile drunk driving arrest rates as a dependent variable to assess the effectiveness of the juvenile zero-tolerance alcohol law, it became necessary to identify how law enforcement efforts and/or the media may have influenced post-intervention changes (if any) in juvenile drunk driving arrest rates.

Changes in law enforcement efforts, regarding the enforcement of this law, and media coverage, especially surrounding the juvenile zero-tolerance alcohol law enactment date, may have impacted arrest rates, which should not be directly attributed to the effects of the law. By conducting informal, semi-structured interviews with law enforcement supervisors and archival research of newspaper coverage about the implementation and enforcement of the juvenile zero-tolerance alcohol law, a general assessment was made to determine if law enforcement efforts and media coverage were plausible threats to the construct and statistical conclusion validity of this research.

In evaluating interrupted time-series designs, the area (time-periods) surrounding the interruption and the observations on and around the enforcement date of the new law, are key in determining trends at the impact point (Mohr, 1988). The observed trends at the interruption site often are attributed to the implementation of the law, but laws are not enacted in a vacuum (Shadish, Cook, & Campbell, 2002). Often, prior to the enforcement of a particular law, law enforcement agencies are provided directives clarifying the law and suggesting implementation strategies (e.g., command directives, prosecutorial notes).

Further, to ensure that societal members are aware of the details of the new law, public service announcements and media coverage precede the enactment of the new law (Hingson et al., 1987; Mueller, 1989; Ross et al., 1981; West et al., 1989). Failure to control for law enforcement efforts and the media impact could mask the true effects of a law's impact (Hingson et al., 1987; Ross et al., 1981; West et al., 1989). "With most simple interrupted time-series designs, the major threat to internal validity is history – the possibility that forces other than the treatment under investigation influenced the dependent variable at the same time at which the intervention was introduced" (Shadish et al., 2002, p. 179).

Through semi-structured informal interviews, law enforcement officials provided specific information pertaining to changes in administrative procedures (instrumentation validity), budget information, manpower, primary focus of enforcement efforts, and task force information which assisted in explaining trends in the data. Further, law enforcement officials and the archival data were used to assist in determining at what point the intervention began. Although the law was officially enforceable on August 01, 1996, pre-enforcement efforts (e.g., media highlights and courtesy traffic stops/verbal warnings) or delayed enforcement efforts (e.g., pending clarification or funding) were addressed by law enforcement officials and assisted in identifying any intervention diffusion. Local newspapers also were screened for any historical events that may have had an impact on the pre- and post-intervention periods.

Finally, determining police officers' attitudes about enforcing the juvenile drinking and driving law also was imperative to understanding the data. It is crucial to remember that the zero-tolerance juvenile drinking and driving law was forced on the states by the federal government through the threat of reduction in highway construction funds. Pennsylvania legislators did not initiate the zero-tolerance juvenile drinking and driving law and the lower BAC levels. If the legislation was not deemed necessary by law enforcement agencies within the commonwealth, other than to secure federal highway funding, there may be little emphasis on enforcing the lower BAC standards established for juveniles in regards to drinking and driving.

The addition of these qualitative components, combined with multiple interrupted time-series models, produced a more potentially valid measure of the impact of the law, than would be anticipated by merely conducting a statistical analysis of arrest rates or fatality accidents. Failures to control for law enforcement and media effects could cause attributions to the law that were not justified.

Interrupted Time-Series (ITS)

Interrupted Time-Series Designs

The quantitative component of this proposed research utilized an interrupted time-series design (ITS) to evaluate the effectiveness of Pennsylvania's zero-tolerance juvenile driving while intoxicated law. The ITS analysis provided a description of the difference between reality and the counterfactual. In simpler terms, it was the difference between what really happened after an intervention and what would have been projected to happen had the intervention not occurred. The projection of what did not occur (counterfactual) was based on the pattern identified by the pre-intervention data (Mohr, 1988). ITS is an effective design for evaluating the impact of various types of laws and interventions (Britt, Kleck, & Bordua, 1996; Katz, Webb, & Schaeffer, 2001; Krimmel & Mele, 1998; Moody & Marvell, 1996; Reynolds, Seydlitz, & Jenkins, 2000) and especially the effects of drinking age laws (Evans et al., 1991; Figlio, 1995; Muller, 1989; Shore & Maguin, 1988; West et al., 1989).

Numerous dependent variables were used to examine the impact of Pennsylvania's zero-tolerance juvenile drunk driving law. The variables were: 1) juvenile drunk driving rates of arrest in Ohio and PA; 2) adult drunk driving rates of arrest in PA; 3) juvenile alcohol related arrests other than drunk driving in PA; and, 4) juvenile alcohol and non-alcohol related fatality traffic accidents rates in Ohio and PA. All of the variables were measured from January 1990 through December 2003, with the exception of Ohio's juvenile drunk driving arrest rates. The data was not available for this variable prior to June 1993.

The research methodology used complimentary ITS models as checks against each other, in an attempt to identify and control for issues involving internal validity, external validity, statistical conclusion validity, and construct validity. DUI juvenile and adult arrest data was obtained from the Pennsylvania UCR database and the Ohio State Highway Patrol (OSHP). A limitation to these data is that all the law enforcement agencies in Pennsylvania and Ohio do not contribute data to the UCR system or the OSHP. However, this did not pose a great systematic bias because the contributors to these databases remain constant.

The three preferred methods of characterizing changes in an ITS design are: 1) visual inspection; 2) regression analysis; and, 3) autoregressive moving average models (ARIMA) (Mohr, 1988). The primary analysis method used was visual analysis, supported by ARIMA modeling.

Underlying Theoretical Conceptualizations

Deterrence Ideology

Pennsylvania uses the threat of legal sanctions in an attempt to deter juveniles from consuming alcohol. These sanctions, which include monetary fines, driver's license revocation, parental notification, and possible imprisonment, are based on rational choice/deterrence theory. From a rational choice perspective, laws and policies with severe violation penalties should be effective in deterring juveniles from drinking alcohol, provided the juveniles perceive that there is substantial certainty of getting both caught and punished.

One would posit that juveniles, after assessing the benefits of consuming alcohol compared to the repercussions of getting caught, would rationally refrain from drinking, and especially from drinking and driving. However, the inability of deterrence-based legislation to dissuade juveniles from drinking and driving is thoroughly documented (Corbett & Simon, 1992; Erickson et al., 1977; Grasmick & Bursik, 1990; Lanza-Kaduce, 1988; Paternoster, 1989; Pogarsky, 2002; Tibbetts, 1997).

Remember, the perceived need for the zero-tolerance juvenile driving while intoxicated legislation was the failure of another deterrence-based policy, the Federal Uniform Drinking Age Act of 1984, which prohibits any juvenile from consuming alcohol. Further, other theoretical perspectives dispute or cast doubt on the veracity of deterrence theory, especially in its ability to deter alcohol related offenses and juveniles.

Conflicting Theories

The effectiveness of deterrent-based legislation to reduce juvenile drinking and driving is brought into question by several other theoretical perspectives. From a psychosocial approach: drunk driving, risky driving, and delinquent behavior within juveniles all are highly correlated with risk taking and low self-control (Donovan, 1993; Shope & Bingham, 2002). Individuals with low self-control lack the capacity to look at the long-term repercussions of their immediate actions (Gottfredson & Hirschi, 1990). From a psychosocial perspective, any attempts to reduce juvenile alcohol use would not include increasing the punishment for offending, since this arguably only enhances the excitement of offending, which is actually the thrill offenders are seeking when they partake in high risk behaviors.

Psychological and psycho-physiological perspectives also predict that a deterrence approach, such as a zero-tolerance alcohol law, may fail to deter juveniles from committing alcohol related offenses (Evans et al., 1991; Muller, 1989; Perkins, Meilman, Leichliter, Cashin, & Presley, 1999; West et al., 1989). Alcohol use is perceived by juveniles as a means of socialization and as a right of passage to adulthood, similar to voting, serving in the armed forces, and driving an automobile. Developmental theories would predict that violating statutory laws would become a motivational factor for adolescent-limited offenders who are seeking adult status (Moffitt, 1993).

Cognitive disruption theories suggest that after consuming alcohol, juveniles lack the ability to make rational choices. The alcohol affects their cognitive decision making processes and they fail to identify the long-term consequences of their immediate actions (Chermack & Giancola, 1997). The chemical effects of alcohol not only slow down reaction time and act as a general depressant on the body, but alcohol also affects executive cognitive functions (ECF). "The ECF govern higher order cognitive abilities such as reasoning, problem solving, attention, planning, and regulating behavior in accordance with anticipated consequences" (Exum, 2002, p. 937). The consumption of a sufficient quantity of alcohol negates the ability to make a rational decision.

Theories other than those founded on rational choice and deterrence offer valuable insight as to why legislative attempts based on deterrence doctrine may be ineffective in preventing juveniles from drinking and driving. They also highlight the need to evaluate the legislation to determine if it provided the desired results, a reduction in juvenile drunk driving offenders and juvenile alcohol-related traffic accident fatalities.

Summary

The impact of zero-tolerance juvenile drinking and driving laws is difficult to predict. As a whole, the U.S. society places little emphasis on the general issue of juvenile alcohol consumption (Jacobs, 1989; Johnston, O'Malley,

Bachman, & Schulenberg, 2004; Levy, 2002; PCCD, 2004; Perkins et al., 1999). Laws that are not supported by strong societal norms often are disobeyed regardless of the legal sanctions (Tittle & Logan, 1973). In contrast, the U.S. society is extremely sensitive to incidents of drunk driving, whether involving juveniles or adults (Donovan, 1993; Jacobs, 1989; Levy, 2002). Laws that are created around strong societal norms often are adhered to based on the fear of social and personal repercussions, regardless of the threatened legal sanctions (Tittle & Logan, 1973).

Acknowledging the difference in U.S. societal attitudes between juvenile alcohol consumption and those regarding drinking and driving, the question remains, what was the impact of Pennsylvania's zero-tolerance approach, using a deterrence-based law, in preventing juveniles from drinking and driving? While the consistent reliance on policy based on a questionable theoretical foundation is a complex issue, part of what seems to be occurring relates to how the effectiveness of this legislation should be assessed (e.g., decline in juvenile alcohol related fatalities, increase in juvenile arrest rates for drunk driving, a decrease in juvenile arrest rates for drunk driving, etc.).

This research about the effects of Pennsylvania's zero-tolerance approach to deterring juvenile drunk driving attempted to identify and describe the impact of the law. For this research the law's impact was evaluated using multiple variables, which will offer a more accurate interpretation of the law's effects.

The use of four ITS models (simple, nonequivalent no-treatment control group, switching replication, and a nonequivalent dependent variable), combined with knowledge of the media and enforcement efforts significantly added credibility to the research findings. The

ITS models not only triangulated the data amongst themselves, but data trends were further supported/explained by the addition of interviews with law enforcement personnel and media information. The integration of the qualitative and quantitative research paradigms offered a more holistic understanding of the information displayed by the ITS models and offered valuable insight about the impact of Pennsylvania's zero-tolerance approach to juvenile drinking and driving.

Chapter 2

The History of DUI Legislation

The purpose of this research was to assess the impact of Pennsylvania's zero-tolerance juvenile drinking and driving law. This literature review briefly describes deterrence theory, which is the theoretical foundation for this law. The theoretical summary is followed by a review of research findings about the effects of drinking and driving laws passed in other states, and on the effectiveness of deterring drinking and driving in general. Finally, additional empirical research is reviewed that has questioned the validity of taking a legislative or deterrent approach in an attempt to reduce juvenile drinking and driving.

Before proceeding, it is important to note that deterrence theory is not addressed in great detail in this literature review for three reasons. First, the impact of the law is being assessed, not its theoretical foundation. Second, the space afforded for this literature review is inadequate to address deterrence theory in immense detail. Finally, Beccaria (1764/1986) explicit warns against using deterrence theory in an attempt to control virtues and vices, arguing that laws alone will not change human behavior. Consequently, the review of deterrence theory is offered to provide a foundation and context for the evaluation of the zero-tolerance law and its impact.

Deterrence Doctrine

Assumptions

Arguably, the principle of using the fear of positive and negative sanctions in an attempt to reinforce and/or shape behavior in humans has been practiced since the beginning of human history. Based on this principle, Cesare Beccaria established the foundation for deterrence theory when he wrote his classic essay *On Crimes and Punishment* (1764/1986). In this essay, Beccaria made several assumptions about human nature. He believed that all people possess free will, in essence, the ability to decide whether to commit or refrain from committing any act, to include crimes. Along with free will, was the assumption that people were capable of making rational decisions and selecting appropriate alternatives. Beccaria also believed that humankind was hedonistic and that without laws they would seek personal pleasure oblivious to how their actions impacted on others within their society (Beccaria, 1764/1986).

Beccaria's (1764/1986) final supposition is based on his first three assumptions. If humans do possess freewill, are capable of rational thoughts, and will seek individual pleasure, societal members must be controlled through the threat of negative sanctions. He believed that for society to function effectively, crimes (as identified by a social consensus) and their associated punishments had to be identified in writing and publicized so each person within the society could make a rational decision based on accurate information. Further, violations of societal laws should be punished based on the harm caused to society, and if caught, both the offender and societal members would witness certain, proportionately severe, and prompt punishment.

Deterrence Research

Deterrence theory is possibly the most tested of all theories in criminology (Akers, 2000), and has been the primary subject of several books (Archambeault, 1979; Beccaria, 1764/1986; Bishop, 1982; Gibbs, 1975; Hagan, 1982; Zimring & Hawkins, 1973). Continued interest in deterrence theory, and individual offenders, has resulted in Beccaria's deterrence concepts being operationalized using a multitude of definitions and perceptions in an attempt to identify offenders' motivations and decision-making capacities/processes (Paternoster, 1989; Piquero & Paternoster, 1998; Piquero & Rengert, 1999; Pogarsky, 2002; Stafford & Warr, 1993). Arguably, Beccaria's straightforward (and likely oversimplified) philosophy about deterrence has become extremely complicated when assessed in current criminological research.

Deterrence theory, which hypothesizes that offenders will be deterred from committing criminal acts if the punishment for the crime outweighs the pleasure gained from committing the crime, presents a false impression of parsimony. Research on deterrence theory has identified that the concepts of pleasure and pain are not linear, in that as punishments increase, crimes do not necessarily decrease (Tittle & Logan, 1973; Zimring & Hawkins, 1973). Further, the assumptions about human nature made by Beccaria (1764/1986), especially the ability of humans to make rational decisions, has developed into elaborate assessment models, which encompass offenders' perceptions and personal/vicarious experiences; different types of deterrence (marginal, restrictive, absolute, general, and specific); and the effects of legal, social, and personal sanctions as perceived by the potential offender (Erickson et al., 1977; Paternoster, 1989; Piquero & Paternoster, 1998; Piquero & Rengert, 1999; Pogarsky, 2002; Saltzman et al., 1982; Stafford & Warr, 1993). In providing the following simplistic overview of the theory, the reader is cautioned not to negate the complexity of attempting to regulate human behavior, and even morality, through threats of punishment.

Swiftness of Punishment

"The more prompt the punishment is and the sooner it follows the crime, the more just and useful it will be" (Beccaria, 1764/1986, p. 36). The need for swift punishment is so the pain inflicted by the punishment is directly associated, by the offender and society, to the crime that was perpetrated. "...for the less time that passes between the misdeed and its chastisement, the stronger and more permanent is the human mind's association of the two ideas of *crime and punishment*, so that imperceptibly the one will come to be considered as the cause and the other as the necessary and inevitable result" (Beccaria, 1764/1986, p. 36).

However, those studies that have assessed the impact of celerity in legal sanctions report little or no empirical support for the proposition that an increase in celerity is effective as a specific or general deterrent to future offending (e.g., Legge & Park, 1994; Nagin & Pogarsky, 2001; Yu, 1994). Nagin & Pogarsky (2001) note: "punishment imminence (celerity) has been accorded co-equal status with certainty and severity in theory, yet empirical tests of the celerity effect are scant" (p. 865). The lack of empirical support for the proposition that swiftly imposed legal punishment will provide a specific and general deterrence from criminal activity has caused this concept to be dropped from most evaluations of deterrence theory (Nagin & Pogarsky, 2001; Paternoster & Bachman, 2001; Piquero & Rengert, 1999).

One observation, not found in the research literature, is that while research about the deterrent effects for the perceived certainty and severity of punishment have advanced into the realms of self-imposed and social sanctions, research on the deterrent effects of celerity have remained focused solely on the impact of legal sanctions (e.g., Donohew et al., 1999; Lanza-Kaduce, 1988; Paternoster, 1989; Pogarsky, 2002; Tibbetts, 1997). Arguably, self-imposed and social sanctions are applied more rapidly than legal sanctions and do affect human behavior (Pogarsky, 2002; Tibbetts, 1997). A strong argument could be made that support for the stronger deterrent effects observed in measures of self-imposed and social sanctions, as compared to legal sanctions (Grasmick & Bursick, 1990; Piquero & Paternoster, 1998; Tibbetts, 1997) is partially accredited to the immediacy of punishment (e.g., guilt, shame, loss of respect, etc.). For example, if guilt, shame, or loss of respect could be deferred, would the correlation between the perceived certainty and/or severity of self-imposed/social sanctions and the intent to commit criminal/deviant acts be weakened?

Severity

The punishment must fit the crime, in that the punishment for a crime must be proportionate to the harm that the crime caused to society (Beccaria, 1764/1986). If the threatened pain to be inflicted by the punishment fails in comparison to the anticipated pleasure, deterrence of that particular offense will be unsuccessful. For example, prior to Pennsylvania's enactment of the zero-tolerance juvenile drinking and driving law, a juvenile who had consumed alcohol, but had a Blood Alcohol Concentration (BAC) under .10 mg/ml, was charged with unlawful consumption of alcohol. The operation of a motor vehicle while under the legal limit for intoxication did not enhance the severity of the punishment. In an attempt to deter juveniles from operating a motor vehicle after consuming any alcohol, the zero-tolerance law, along with its more severe charge (driving while intoxicated) and increased sanctions, was enacted.

If the punishment is too severe for the harm that the crime caused to society, the certainty of punishment will be negated through other means (Beccaria, 1764/1986). An example in support of Beccaria's belief is when the speed limit in the United States was established at 55 mph on all interstates. With severe penalties for speeding, many law enforcement jurisdictions failed to enforce the 55 mph speed limit. The lack of societal support, along with minimum enforcement, eventually lead to the law being repealed. Similarly, law enforcement officers may believe that the zero-tolerance juvenile alcohol policy punishment is too severe and may charge juveniles with lesser offenses, which involve less paperwork, less patrol officer hours, and avoid mandatory court appearances (Olivero, Hansen, & Clark, 1993). McLaughlin (1985) reported that few police officers had a strong moralistic or punitive view towards individuals who were intoxicated. "For most, punishment in general, and the use of the criminal law in particular, was seen as both an ineffective and inappropriate response to drunkenness" (p. 357).

Empirical research has found little or no support for the severity of legal sanctions to deter offenders (Paternoster, 1989, 1987; Piliavin, Thornton, Gartner, & Matsueda,

1986; Sherman & Weisburd, 1995; Ward & Tittle, 1993). An explanation as to why there appears to be a lack of empirical support for the severity of legal sanctions to deter offenders is offered by Piliavin et al.:

> We are suggesting that persons' evaluations or imputed meanings of sanctions are important in determining their behavior. These evaluations or meanings may be conditioned by elements within the immediate situation confronting the individual. For example the persons' perceptions of the opportunity, returns, and support for crime within a given situation may influence perceptions of risks and the extent to which those risks are discounted. This implies that the effective assessments of risk are to some extent situationally-induced, transitory, and unstable (1986, p. 115-116).

The lack of support for the severity of sanctions to deter some offenders may be correlated with the individual's perception of the certainty of punishment. If individuals perceive there is little or no chance of getting caught or prosecuted, they can immediately discount the severity of punishment component of deterrence theory. "The certainty of a chastisement, even if it be moderate, will always make a greater impression than the fear of a more terrible punishment that is united with the hope of impunity;...especially if that hope is reinforced by the examples of impunity..." (Beccaria, 1764/1986, p. 46).

Certainty

Beccaria (1764/1986) limited his discussion about the certainty of punishment to the enforcement of sanctions once an individual was sentenced. He observed the certainty that a moderate punishment would be imposed was of greater deterrence value to the offender and the public than extremely cruel punishments, which were not enforced. Seldom has recent research operationalized the certainty variable solely as the certainty that the offender would be punished (e.g., Pogarsky, 2002). Most often, the certainty component of deterrence theory is operationalized by multiple variables, which attempt to account for both the certainty of punishment and the certainty of arrest/getting caught (e.g., Erickson et al., 1977; Grasmick & Bursik, 1990; Paternoster, 1987; Piliavin et al., 1986; Piquero & Rengert, 1999), or measured solely as the certainty of arrest/getting caught (e.g., Brown, 1978; Paternoster, 1989; Piquero & Paternoster, 1998; Saltzman et al., 1982; Scheider, 2001; Sherman & Weisburd, 1995; Tittle & Rowe, 1974).

Regardless of how current research measures the perceived certainty of punishment, either as arrest and/or as sentencing, the variable often is found to be the most significant component within the deterrence theory in deterring individuals from committing criminal acts. As an individual's perception of being arrested or sanctioned increases, his/her intent of offending decreases (Paternoster, 1987; Piquero & Paternoster, 1998; Sherman & Weisburd, 1995). Current research offers minimum to moderate support for the negative correlation that exists between the perceived certainty of getting caught for committing an offense and actually committing the offense (Grasmick & Bursik, 1990; Piliavin et al., 1986; Piquero & Paternoster, 1998; Piquero & Rengert, 1999; Scheider, 2001; Saltzman et al., 1982; Sherman & Weisburd, 1995).

Although the zero-tolerance juvenile drinking and driving law drastically increased the severity of punishment for juvenile drivers who have consumed alcohol, the law did little to enhance the perceived certainty of detection. If authorized and adequately funded, the establishment of Driving Under the Influence (DUI) task forces, roadblocks, and other police activities can increase the certainty of identifying and arresting drunk drivers (but these activities were not directly mandated or funded under this law). These police tactics have been shown to have a positive effect in reducing fatality accidents related to drinking and driving, but these effects often are short lived as limited police resources are needed elsewhere (Jacobs, 1989; Ross, 1985; West et al., 1989).

Since the 1980s, the certainty of being stopped by the police for drinking and driving has increased. In the 1980s, it was estimated that only about .001% of those individuals who were driving while legally intoxicated were actually detected by the police (Hingson et al., 1987). In 2000, the estimated detection rate for driving while legally intoxicated had increased to 3% (Hingson & Winter, 2003). The perception of being detected by the police for driving while legally intoxicated also has increased. Survey data from the 1980s indicates that 25% of the respondents perceived that the police would catch them if they attempted to drive while legally intoxicated (Jacobs, 1989). In 2000, the perceived certainty of getting stopped by the police for driving while legally intoxicated had increased to just over 60% (Hingson & Winter, 2003). Although these studies indicate that the perception of getting stopped for drunk driving is increasing, this does not necessarily translate into less drunk driving offenses.

In the same study where the sample perceived there was a 60% chance of getting stopped for drunk driving, they also perceived only a 3% chance of being arrested and convicted if stopped for drunk driving (Hingson and Winter, 2003). For this sample, the perception of being detected for drunk driving was 20 times higher than their perception of being convicted for drunk driving. Thus, the perceived increase in the fear of arrest, which should have reduced drunk driving offenses, is apparently negated by the extremely low perception of the certainty of punishment. Beccaria (1764/1986) hypothesized that for the threat of sanctions to be a deterrent, the sanctions must be perceived as real by societal members, and reinforced to individuals and society through publicized applications.

Deterrence Theory

Beccaria (1764/1986) believed that humans possess freewill, are capable of rational thoughts, and will seek individual pleasure. Based on these assumptions, he hypothesized that societal members must be legally controlled through the threat of well-publicized negative sanctions. He believed that violations of societal laws should be punished, and if caught, both the offender and societal members would witness certain, proportionately severe, and prompt punishment.

Empirical support for deterrence theory is low to moderate, with the certainty or perceived certainty of getting caught having a stronger deterrent effect than either the severity of punishment or the swiftness of punishment (Akers, 2000; Grasmick & Bursik, 1990; Paternoster & Bachman, 2001; Piliavin et al., 1986; Piquero & Paternoster, 1998; Piquero & Rengert, 1999; Scheider, 2001; Saltzman et al., 1982; Sherman & Weisburd, 1995). In an attempt to accurately measure the deterrent effect of various laws on different kinds of people, researchers have found it necessary to clarify and modify Beccaria's original articulated propositions of certainty, proportional severity, and swiftness. The straightforward propositions of deterrence, originally offered by Beccaria, were found to be insufficient in capturing the complexities of human nature in relation to criminal offending (Paternoster & Bachman, 2001).

Deterrence Concept

General and Specific Deterrence

Deterrence has been conceptualized as operating from two different perspectives, specific deterrence and general deterrence (Akers, 2000; Piquero & Paternoster, 1998). Piquero and Paternoster (1998) define general and specific deterrence as:

> Specific deterrence operates when an individual who has committed a crime and has been sanctioned refrains from committing additional criminal acts for fear of another punishment. General deterrence occurs when a would-be offender refrains from committing a crime because another has been punished for offending (p. 3).

Piquero and Paternoster also observed that specific and general deterrence could work simultaneously as an individual is attempting to make a rational decision. "Deterrence appears to involve an intricate mixture of both specific and general deterrence mechanisms" (p. 18).

For the threat of punishment to be a deterrent, and for a would-be offender to make a rational decision, Beccaria (1864/1986) believed that crimes, and their associated punishments, had to be identified in writing and publicized, so each person within the society could make a rational decision based on accurate information. An NHTSA sponsored survey (NHTSA, 2003b) found that 66% of their participants who were between the ages of 16 and 20 were unaware that there was a difference in BAC levels for juveniles as compared to BAC levels established for adults to substantiate drunk driving. Hingson and Winter (2003) found that 56% of the respondents in their national survey, who were age 16 – 20, were not aware of the juvenile zero-tolerance laws in their state. The majority of the respondents were under the assumption that the legal BAC limit to be charged for drinking and driving as a juvenile was the same as the BAC limit established for adults. Although ignorance of the law is not a justification for violating it, for deterrence theory to function, societal members must know the laws and their associated punishments to make a rational decision as whether or not to offend.

Experiential Effect

Each person possesses their own perception about the severity of punishments and the certainty of being arrested and/or punished for committing a particular offense. Four critical areas that support these perceptions are: 1) personal experience with punishment, 2) vicarious experience with punishment, 3) personal experience with punishment avoidance, and 4) vicarious experience with punishment avoidance (Gerrard, Gibbons, Benthin, & Hessling, 1996; Piquero & Paternoster, 1998; Stafford & Warr, 1993).

If individuals have had personal or vicarious experience with punishment, it should increase their perception of being caught and presumably would result in their refraining from the commission of a crime. Conversely, if they have committed a specific offense on several occasions without being caught, their perception of being caught should be diminished and would result in continued or even increased offending. Piquero and Paternoster

(1998) concluded that although this concept was logical, it was not always true. They noted that "our experiences, both personal and vicarious, have mixed effects" (p. 18).

Research findings support the assumption that some individuals, who have been arrested for various offenses, believe that if they had committed the offense ten times before getting arrested, they can commit the same offense another ten times before getting arrested again (Piquero & Paternoster, 1998; Pogarsky & Piquero, 2003). Piquero & Paternoster (1998) noted that one's own experience with vicarious punishment and punishment avoidance for drinking and driving reacted contrary to the predicted effect. Individuals who had friends arrested for drinking and driving were not deterred from committing the offense themselves, and those who had friends who had avoided punishment for drinking and driving were reluctant to commit the offense themselves. They concluded that personal and vicarious experience with punishment and punishment avoidance impacts each individual's decision-making process differently.

Measuring Deterrence

Grasmick and Bursik (1990) note, "conventional deterrence theory focuses attention on state-imposed legal sanctions in the form of physical and material deprivation" (p. 839). However, they found that state-imposed legal sanctions are not the only factors involved in the rational decision-making process. Grasmick and Bursik found that socially imposed costs, such as loss of respect, and self-imposed costs, such as shame and guilt, also affect the decision-making process. They argue that these internal factors can act as a deterrent even if the potential offenders perceive they will not be caught. Additional research supports these findings (Paternoster, 1987; Tibbetts, 1997).

Paternoster (1987) noted that the threat of social and self-imposed sanctions often were sufficient to deter potential offenders. He argues that rational decision-making cannot be restricted to only the deterrence concept (legal sanctions) since social sanctions are part of the decision-making process. Limiting rational decision-making to the certainty and severity of legal sanctions fails to take into account the effects of social and personal sanctions.

Deterrence Research Summary

Current research on deterrence theory is far removed from the simple concepts envisioned by Beccaria (1764/1986), who believed that humans could be deterred from committing crime based on the fear of certain, proportionately severe, and swift legal sanctions. Current research has expanded the deterrence model to include not only legal sanctions, but also the effects of general and specific deterrence, as well as social (e.g., community, parental, and peer sanctions) and personal (e.g., shame and guilt) sanctions (Gerrard et al., 1996; Grasmick & Bursik, 1990; Piquero & Paternoster, 1998; Pogarsky & Piquero, 2003; Stafford & Warr, 1993; Tibbetts, 1997; William & Gibbs, 1981).

Current research has identified idiosyncrasies in both individuals and society, which can affect the effectiveness of deterrent-based legislation. From an individual perspective, experiential effects must be assessed. Specific and general deterrence may deter those individuals who perceive a high certainty of getting caught (personal and vicarious punishment), while those individuals who perceive a low certainty of getting caught (personal and vicarious punishment avoidance) may be motivated to offend (Piquero & Paternoster, 1998; Stafford & Warr,

1993), although this does not hold true for each individual (Piquero & Paternoster, 1998).

Social condemnation for violating a law often is perceived by would-be offenders as a greater deterrent than legal sanctions (Grasmick & Bursik, 1990; Paternoster, 1989; Piquero & Paternoster, 1998; Saltzman et al., 1982; Tittle & Logan, 1973). Thus, laws that are not supported by strong societal norms and have little or no social condemnation attached to their violation are more likely to be disregarded, regardless of the legal sanctions (Tittle & Logan, 1973).

Finally, research suggests that there is little support for increasing the severity and swiftness of punishment for criminal offenses to improve the deterrent impact. The perceived certainty of punishment is the only variable which consistently displays support in relations to deterring individuals from committing criminal offenses, although the relationships tend to be low to moderate at best (Grasmick & Bursik, 1990; Nagin & Paternoster, 1993; Paternoster, 1989, 1987; Piliavin et al., 1986; Sherman & Weisburd, 1995; Ward & Tittle, 1993).

The shortcomings identified in current research about the ineffectiveness of deterrence theory to explain criminal behavior are not without criticism. Gottfredson and Hirschi (1990) suggest that researchers have focused extensively on political sanctions and have failed to acknowledge that the classical criminological model also is comprised of moral, religious, and physical sanctions. They contend that while only political sanctions can define criminal misconduct, the fear generated in an individual from the perceived threat of each of these sanctions define human behavior. Further, these sanctions are so interrelated that they cannot be considered separately.

Classical Criminology and Drinking and Driving

Classical Model

"The troubles of criminology can be traced to the wholesale repudiation of the classical model by the positivist" (Gottfredson & Hirschi, 1990, p. 169). Gottfredson and Hirschi observed that positivist researchers ignored basic assumptions about human nature, which are the foundation of the classical model of criminology. The classical model assumes that it is human nature to seek pleasure and avoid pain. Since this is basic human nature, all people possess the propensity to commit crime (criminality), but the propensity to commit crime is different from the actual commission of a criminal act (Gottfredson & Hirschi, 1990).

By ignoring classical model assumptions about the hedonistic nature of humans, positivists were free to explore their respective fields in an attempt to find the causes of crime and delinquency. The positivists' rejection of the classical model also placed the emphasis of criminology on the violation of legal (political) sanctions, and away from the other types of sanctions identified in the classical model. In an attempt to explain and regulate human behavior, the classical model listed several types of sanctions, which included political sanctions, moral sanctions, religious sanctions, and physical sanctions (Gottfredson & Hirschi, 1990). Political sanctions determine what acts are identified as criminal and non-criminal. Moral sanctions identify what acts are identified by society as deviant and which are conforming. Religious sanctions identify which acts are sinful and which are not, and physical sanctions identify which acts are reckless and those that are cautious or conservative in nature.

Of these four sanctions, political sanctions, because they were imposed on society, punishable by the state, and defined criminal conduct, received the bulk of attention as criminology developed. The lack of emphasis on the other three sanctions has had unfortunate consequences for criminology (Gottfredson & Hirschi, 1990). The unfortunate consequences for criminology are that in focusing primarily on political sanctions, researchers fail to see the correlations among all the sanctions and an individual's behavior. Skinner (1953) notes:

> To show how an individual actually comes to abide by a code, we should have to analyze how he learns not to lie, not to steal, not to assault others, and so on. The governmental agency may codify its controlling practices and maintain the contingencies thus set forth, but it seldom attempts to make the code effective in any other way... In asserting that "ignorance of the law is no excuse," the governmental agency leaves the actual conditioning of the individual to others. Parents and friends establish minor contingencies, which keep behavior within legal bounds, and the governmental function may also be actively supported by the ethical group and by religious and educational institutions (p. 339).

Although only political sanctions can define criminal conduct, all the sanctions define human behavior. "In our view, the common element in crime, deviant behavior, sin, and accident is so overriding that the tendency to treat them as distinct phenomena subject to distinct causes is one of the major intellectual errors of positive thought and is a major cost of the tendency to divide intellectual problems among academic disciplines" (Gottfredson & Hirschi, 1990, p. 10).

Political/Legal Sanctions

"Unfortunately, even in spite of past efforts, all we know in general is that perceptions of the certainty and severity of punishment do not seem to deter trivial and infrequent behaviors of high school and university students" (Paternoster, 1987, p. 214). Paternoster, in reviewing 15 years of deterrence research (1972 – 1986), discovered that perceptual certainty and perceptual severity of punishment often were found to be insignificant in studies, which included independent variables in the models that controlled for social (e.g., moral condemnation, parental notification) and personal sanctions (e.g., shame, guilt). In comparing the various deterrence studies, Paternoster observed mixed findings on the reported effectiveness of legal sanctions to deter certain offenders.

Pogarsky (2002) also found little support for the proposition that an increase in the perceived certainty and/or perceived severity of legal sanctions would deter juveniles from committing the offense of drunk driving. He noted that the least likely to commit the act of drinking and driving were those juveniles who reported being deterred from committing the offense through self and social disapproval (moral sanctions), rather than the threat of legal punishment. These findings are similar to those of Paternoster (1987) in that the threat of social and self-imposed sanctions often was sufficient to deter potential offenders. The findings also support Gottfredson and Hirschi (1990), in that to explain criminal behavior, research must move beyond evaluating only political sanctions to explain human behavior.

Pogarsky (2002) observed that "deterrable" offenders reported that self-disapproval and peer disapproval of alcohol use were significant deterrents to drinking and driving, as were the certainty and severity of legal sanctions. The deterrable respondents also reported that peer support for alcohol use and previous undetected experiences with drunk driving significantly increased the likelihood that they would commit the offense of drunk driving in the future. Finally, Pogarsky discovered that no legal, social, or self-imposed sanctions were identified as significant in deterring the participants identified as "incorrigible." Pogarsky's findings on the participants categorized as incorrigible, supports Beccaria's (1764/1986) realization that no threat of punishment, regardless of certainty and/or severity, would deter all would-be offenders.

Overall, increases in legal sanctions for alcohol use by juveniles have apparently had little or no effect on juvenile alcohol consumption. According to the *2003 PA Youth Survey Report* (PCCD, 2004), from 1989 through 2003, approximately 50% of Pennsylvania's 12th graders reported consuming alcohol in the past 30 days. The PCCD findings mirror the results of the *2003 Monitoring the Future* national data on estimated alcohol use by 12th graders within the United States (Johnston et al., 2004).

Moral Sanctions

"Rules that have moral support are more enforceable by sanctions than are those that lack moral support" (Tittle & Logan, 1973, p. 385). *2003 Monitoring the Future* data (Johnston et al., 2004) reveals that although peer disapproval among 12th graders on "any alcohol consumption" is low, with only 27.2% disapproving, peer disapproval of binge drinking (five or more drinks in a row) on weekdays and weekends is at a record high, 86.3% and 64.2%, respectively.

The lack of peer support for binge drinking is significant since it should increase the perception of social sanctions for those juveniles who abuse alcohol. Research that has shown little support for the certainty and severity of political sanctions in deterring juvenile drinking, has found that peer sanctions, parental attachment, moral beliefs, shame, and peer involvement are significantly correlated with reductions in juvenile drinking and driving, juvenile use of alcohol, and other minor offenses (Donohew et al., 1999; Grasmick & Bursik, 1990; Lanza-Kaduce, 1988; Paternoster, 1989; Piquero & Paternoster, 1998; Pogarsky, 2002; Tibbetts, 1997). "Perhaps the most consistent finding throughout the analysis concerned the effect of moral beliefs. In almost every single model specification, the effect of moral beliefs exerted a significant effect on the outcome variable…and leading inhibitors of projections to drink and drive" (Piquero & Paternoster, 1998, p. 29).

Since the founding of Mothers Against Drunk Driving (MADD) in 1980, more than 2,300 anti-drunk driving laws have been passed in the United States (Hamilton, 2000). With organizations such as MADD highlighting the high costs associated with drinking and driving, there appears to be unprecedented public attention about, and growing moral support against, drinking and driving (Hingson, 1993). In 1997, 56% of the participants in the National Survey on Drinking and Driving supported a BAC of .08 mg/ml or less as the legal limit to establish drunk driving; by 1999 that percentage had increased to 68% (NHTSA, 2003b).

In Pennsylvania, 25 of every 100,000 licensed juvenile drivers were killed while operating a motor vehicle in 1990, 49.7 % of these fatalities involved an intoxicated juvenile driver. The juvenile driver fatality rate declined through 1994 to 20 per 100,000 licensed juvenile drivers. Those fatality vehicle accidents involving intoxicated juvenile drivers also declined to 38.9 % of all the fatality vehicle accidents involving juvenile drivers. In 1995, the juvenile driver fatality rate increased to 25.8 per 100,000 licensed juvenile drivers, while alcohol related juvenile driver fatality rates continued to decline to 29.8 % of the fatality vehicle accidents involving juvenile drivers. The juvenile driver fatality rate continued to increase through 2003, to 35.3 per 100,000 licensed juvenile drivers, with 28.5 % of these accidents being alcohol related (L. Daniels, personal communication, August 31, 2005).

These statistics, along with the increase in perceived and actual certainty of arrest, allude to a moral resurgence against drinking and driving in general, and with a specific goal of reducing juvenile drinking and driving. If public support against drinking and driving continues to grow, moral sanctions may be more effective in deterring juvenile drinking and driving than legal sanctions (Erickson et al., 1977). However, if public support against drinking and driving declines, due to high juvenile arrest rates for low levels of alcohol consumption, the offense may lose its negative social connotations, thus weakening the perceived moral sanctions.

Religious Sanctions

Moral sanctions categorize actions as moral or immoral based on societal and/or cultural standards. Religious sanctions categorize actions as righteous or sinful based on particular religious ideology (Skinner, 1953). Only one study was found that regressed religious activities on drinking liquor (Paternoster, 1989). The study revealed that for this sample, "religious activities" had a negative, but insignificant relationship with "drinking liquor." Although religious activities was not significant in this study, Skinner (1953) notes that religious sanctions would most often include the sale of alcohol, since the consumption of alcohol can lead to sin and temptation (p. 356).

Physical Sanctions

Decisions to act recklessly or to refrain from high-risk activities are the opposing ends of a continuum referred to as physical sanctions. Jacobs (1989) makes a key point about operating a motor vehicle that often is missed or taken for granted. When an individual accepts a vehicle operator's license, s/he enters into a social contract to operate the motor vehicle within the boundaries of the established laws. Other motor vehicle operators, regardless of race, gender, or age, are under the assumption that fellow motorists will adhere to traffic and vehicle regulations.

A relevant issue with drinking and driving is the risk that it places not only on the offender, but also on anyone in the offender's immediate area. As motorists and pedestrians, we entrust each other to control and safely operate motor vehicles that range in weight from 2,000 pounds to 76,000 pounds, which are traveling at speeds in excess of 88 feet per second, and are passing each other within distances in which it would take less than a 1/10th of a second for two vehicles to collide.

When a driver is impaired or intoxicated, s/he places societal members at risk. The risk is compounded when the driver is intoxicated and between the ages of 16 and 20

(NHTSA, 2003b). Research has shown that novice drivers between the ages of 16 and 20 have the highest traffic accident rate, to include fatality accidents (NHTSA, 2003a). Although most of these accidents are caused by inexperience or overconfidence (e.g., failure to maintain a single lane, too fast for road and weather conditions, failure to yield the right of way), just over 5% of fatality traffic accidents involving drivers under the age of 21 are attributed to erratic, reckless, careless, and/or negligible actions (NHTSA, 2003a).

In a study of pub patrons, Corbett & Simon (1992) found that individuals who had driven while intoxicated justified their reckless actions through confidence in their skill and control, convenience, perception of not getting caught, social pressures (passengers, friends, others), and the enjoyment of rule breaking and risk taking. Those who reported refraining from drinking and driving did so because of safety concerns, fear of penalty, impaired judgment, social influences, and the ability to make other transportation arrangements. The reasons offered as justifications for drinking and driving reflect the offenders' self-interests and desire to risk injuries and sanctions, compared to the lack of risk-taking by those who refrained from drinking and driving.

Deterrence Theory and Alcohol Consumption

Sanctions and Drinking and Driving

Numerous studies have assessed the various impacts of juvenile-related alcohol laws (Figlio, 1995; Hilton, 1984; Hingson et al., 1987; Mueller, 1989; Ross et al., 1981; West et al., 1989). Mueller (1989) reported that in Oklahoma, the increase in the legal age to purchase and consume alcohol, from age 18 to 21, had little or no impact on the rate of fatality accidents involving intoxicated juvenile drivers. These findings are contrary to those reported by Figlio (1995), who reported a significant drop in juvenile fatalities in Wisconsin after the drinking age was raised to 21 years of age.

Mueller (1989) observed that the threat of license revocation did have a significant and permanent impact on the intentions to drink and drive. Ross et al. (1981) found the same findings in their drinking and driving study in France, but discovered the effect to be temporary, slowly dissipating after one year. Ross et al. noted that initially the law had a positive impact in reducing drinking and driving arrests and fatality accidents involving alcohol. The law was well advertised and the threat of apprehension was increased through mandatory breathalyzer tests for all motorists passing through established checkpoints. "Our explanation of why the deterrent effect was lost is that the threat was not fulfilled and the people gradually learned this fact" (p. 366). Hingson et al. (1987) described findings identical to those witnessed by Ross et al.

Hingson et al. (1987) assessed the effects of Maine's 1981 and Massachusetts' 1982 drinking and driving laws using interrupted time-series designs. They found that prior to the implementation of the law, fatality accidents in both states had started to decline. Hingson et al. attributed the pre-intervention decline in traffic fatalities to heavy media coverage of both the new legislation and the perceived social concern associated with drinking and driving. The researchers also observed that there appeared to be a trade-off in the cause of fatality accidents. As law enforcement officers were assigned to checkpoints and DUI task forces, they were removed from traffic duty. The issuance of speeding citations dropped 44% from the time the law was implemented in 1981, until 1984 (31,045 and

19,693, respectively). Speeding is considered the single most contributing factor in fatality traffic accidents (NHTSA, 2003a). Hingson et al. speculate that the lives saved through enforcement of the drinking and driving laws may have been negated by those lost as a result of speeding.

West et al. (1989) found that when jail sentences and suspension of drivers' licenses were mandated for first time DUI offenders in Arizona, the rate of fatality traffic accidents in that state dropped abruptly and remained semi-permanent. "We also note that the estimated rate of decay of the effectiveness of the Arizona and California laws was much slower than has typically been found in previous evaluations of the effectiveness of harsher penalties for drunk driving, even bordering on a permanent effect" (p. 1233).

Hilton (1984), who conducted the study about the impact of California's drunk driving laws, found results similar to those of West et al. (1989), in that fatality accidents involving alcohol dropped significantly after the drunk driving laws were implemented. Hilton also noted that non-alcohol related traffic fatalities dropped at a rate similar to those involving alcohol. Hilton concluded "results that indicated deterrence were not found where they were most expected" (p. 625). In other words, since the law was not intended to lower non-alcohol related traffic fatalities, there was the strong plausibility of a third variable, which impacted both alcohol related and non-alcohol related traffic fatality rates.

Overall, research indicates that the threat of increased legal sanctions as a means to deter juvenile drinking and driving is at best marginally effective. Even in those studies where a significant deterrent effect was observed, it was demonstrated to either be a temporary effect that slowly dissipated over time or an effect that also was mirrored in variables which the law should not have affected, suggesting a plausible third variable. Ross (1982) reported the same findings when he evaluated drinking and driving legislation that was implemented in Scandinavia, Great Britain, France, The Netherlands, New Zealand, Australia, and Canada. Ross concluded that the temporary deterrent effect initially observed was because of a raised awareness in drivers' perceptions that the certainty of getting caught had increased, based on the media effects surrounding the implementation of these various drinking and driving laws. When the certainty of arrest did not manifest, drinking and driving rates and fatality accidents involving intoxicated drivers returned to pre-intervention levels. Although the threat of more severe legal sanctions have failed to deter adults from drinking and driving, it is possible, but not very plausible, that such sanctions could deter juveniles from drinking and driving.

Sanctions and Alcohol Consumption by Juveniles

Using surveys and scenario generated questions, many studies have attempted to identify which variables, if any, were significantly related to juvenile alcohol consumption and juvenile drunk driving (Corbett & Simon, 1992; Erickson et al., 1977; Grasmick & Bursik, 1990; Paternoster, 1989; Pogarsky, 2002; Tibbetts, 1997). Pogarsky (2002) modeled a research design based on the concept of marginal deterrence. Marginal deterrence is the identification of the amount of deterrence necessary to prevent the majority of societal members from committing a particular offense (Zimring & Hawkins, 1968). He used this concept to develop a typology for drinking and driving offenders. He identified three categories of individuals: 1) acute conformist, 2) deterrable offender, and 3) the incorrigible offender.

The acute conformist refrains from drinking and driving based on personal and social ideology, often not considering the punishments threatened by law. Paternoster (1987) described this type of offender with the following example when discussing marijuana use: "Because the social and occupational costs are so high, I (and many like me) do not even take the next step and evaluate the threat posed by formal legal sanctions" (p. 211).

The incorrigible offender is identified as an individual who will not be deterred from offending regardless of the certainty or severity of sanctions. Beccaria (1764/1986) noted that "…human laws cannot prevent disturbances and disorders amid the infinite and utterly conflicting attractions of pleasure and pain" (p. 74).

Deterrable offenders are the people who are not so strongly bound to society that they will refrain from drinking and driving based solely on morals and/or the threat of informal sanctions (Pogarsky, 2002). Theoretically, deterrable offenders need laws and the threat of punishment to deter them from offending. To reference an old adage, "a lock is intended to keep an honest person honest." If society were comprised only of acute conformists, there would be no need for locks. A lock will not deter the incorrigible, who will force the lock open. The lock's purpose is to deter the deterrable, those who without the lock's presence may be tempted to commit a criminal offense.

In his sample of 412 college students, Pogarsky (2002) observed that 21% were categorized as acute conformists, 62% were categorized as deterrable, and 8% were categorized as incorrigible (9% were not categorized). Using multiple regression, Pogarsky found that for the acute conformists and the deterrable offenders, a significant negative relationship existed between certainty of punishment, severity of punishment, and self-disapproval when regressed against the likelihood of drinking and driving. For these same two groups, having committed the offense of drinking and driving in the past had a significant positive relationship with the likelihood to commit the offense in the future. For the incorrigibles, no formal or informal sanctions were identified as significant with the likelihood that they would refrain from drinking and driving in the future. Overall, the research displayed that 38% (157 out of 412) of the sample were not discouraged by the threat of legal sanctions for drinking and driving. The percentage of those who were not deterred by legal sanctions for drinking and driving was similar to that reported by Corbett & Simon (1992).

Paternoster (1989), in evaluating juvenile alcohol consumption, found that the perceived certainty and severity of sanctions were not a deterrent. Similar to Pogarsky (2002), Paternoster identified that those high school students who possessed high moral beliefs and feared the repercussion of peer sanctions were deterred from future alcohol consumption. Paternoster also found that prior alcohol use and associating with peers who approved of alcohol use significantly reinforced the continued use of alcohol.

Tibbetts (1997) conducted a study about drinking and driving using a sample of college undergraduates. He found support for moral beliefs and shame as significant deterrents to drinking and driving. The research also displayed that low self-control (Grasmick scale, 1993), pleasure (fun of committing the act), and prior offending were significantly related to future intentions of offending. Tibbetts' findings support those reported earlier by Grasmick & Bursik (1990).

The difference in Grasmick and Bursik (1990) and Tibbetts's (1997) research, as compared to the others reviewed here, is that these two studies found support that legal sanctions were a significant deterrent for drinking and driving. In Tibbetts's research, "external sanctions" included both legal (certainty of arrest) and social sanctions (university dismissal, family and friend detection), which were summed into a composite score. The significance of purely legal sanctions could not be segregated from the impact of the social sanctions, which could account for the significant finding.

Another possible explanation for these mixed findings is the geographical areas where the research was conducted. Geographical areas often have distinct social and cultural environments. Whether the residents of a particular geographical area condone or condemn juvenile alcohol consumption and juvenile drunk driving may influence both the proclivity and the enforcement of these offenses. Skinner (1953) notes: "Behavior comes to conform to the standards of a given community when certain responses are reinforced and others are allowed to go unreinforced or are punished" (p. 415). Skinner offers as an example the conflict juveniles confront in premarital sexual relations, where religious and governmental agencies cling to older cultural values of abstinence, but communities and families have accepted a more informative/educational approach. His example appears transferable to juvenile alcohol consumption, where juveniles also receive conflicting cultural messages about alcohol use (Levy, 2002; Marks, Graham, & Hansen, 1992; Moffitt, 1993; PCCD, 2004; Perkins et al., 1999).

Juvenile Drinking and Driving Offenders

Lanza-Kaduce (1988) in studying the reasons why juveniles committed the offense of drunk driving noted:

> Social definitions and sanctions rather than legal ones may provide the reinforcement contingencies for learning both the behavior and favorable definitions about it.... Some youths positively define and are rewarded for risk-taking. Taking risks with legal punishment (and drunk driving) may meet the expectations and gain the approval of friends. This may address why many respondents drink and drive despite perceiving it as risky (p. 335).

These findings are supported by research about juvenile drinking and driving conducted by Shope & Bingham (2002) and Donovan (1993), and support the propositions found in self-control theory (Gottfredson & Hirschi, 1990).

In brief, self-control theory is a micro-level criminological theory based on soft determinism. Although individuals are not born naturally evil or naturally good, unless properly socialized, they will lack self-control and will be more prone to commit crime, deviance, sin, and reckless acts. Self-control is a learned activity, which becomes relatively stable after age eight (Gottfredson & Hirschi, 1990).

A child who is not taught self-control will be more prone to seek pleasure and to avoid pain by committing acts of force or fraud undertaken in pursuit of self-interest (crime). Individuals who possess low self-control will tend to be more impulsive, physical, risk-taking, short sighted, nonverbal, and insensitive, but will not necessarily be criminals, although they will be more likely to commit criminal, deviant, sinful, and reckless acts if provided the opportunity (Gottfredson & Hirschi, 1990).

In researching behavioral and psychosocial correlates to drinking and driving, Donovan (1993) discovered that those juveniles who reported drinking and driving scored significantly higher on measures of verbal aggression, physical aggression, and risk-taking. Further, juveniles who reported drinking and driving also scored significantly higher on measures of risky driving (e.g., speeding, passing and following violations, and control signal violations), as well as being significantly more likely to operate a vehicle after taking drugs other than alcohol. Donovan concluded that those juveniles who routinely drove after drinking alcohol: 1) tended to violate other traffic laws; 2) had problem behaviors in general; and 3) tended to be risk-takers, and were somewhat more aggressive/hostile than those who refrained from drinking and driving.

Shope and Bingham (2002), using longitudinal data, found that their results mirrored those identified by Donovan (1993). They concluded "drinking and driving is a component of problem behavior…Young people who drink and drive also report more drinking problems, drug use, and delinquent behavior" (p. 32).

These findings (Donovan, 1993; Lanza-Kaduce, 1988; Shope & Bingham, 2002) all support the propositions of low self-control theory as described by Gottfredson and Hirschi (1990). Donovan (1993) concluded that the intent to commit the offense of drunk driving is not an isolated decision, but manifests from "a larger lifestyle reflecting behavioral and psychosocial unconventionality" (p. 601).

These findings further suggest that it will be difficult, using only the threat of increased punishment, to reduce drinking and driving in juveniles who exhibit "behavioral and psychosocial unconventionality," since sanctions only enhance the risk, which these particular juveniles already are willing to take (Donovan, 1993; Shope & Bingham, 2002).

Rival Theories

Developmental Theory

Moffitt (1993) and Arnett (2000) identified similar behavioral patterns in adolescents, and attributed the behavior as a product of adolescent development. Moffitt identified two types of adolescent offenders, the life-course-persistent and the adolescent-limited. The life-course-persistent offender is similar in behavior to Pogarsky's (2002) incorrigible offender. The adolescence-limited offender is similar in character to the deterrable offender.

Moffitt (1993) suggests "the origins of adolescence-limited delinquency lie in youngsters' best efforts to cope with the widening gap between biological and social maturity" (p. 692). Moffitt also predicts that adolescence-limited offenders will engage in crimes "that symbolize adult privilege or that demonstrate autonomy from parental control" (p. 695). These types of offenses would include alcohol use and drunk driving. Alcohol use is a status offense, only illegal by the virtue of age, or in this case underage. Similarly, the zero-tolerance drinking and driving legislation signifies to adolescence-limited offenders that their actions are illegal only because of their age, assuming that they are operating a motor vehicle with a BAC of less than .08 mg/ml.

Arnett (2000) agrees with the developmental approach, but suggests that with emerging adulthood comes the need for risk-taking (e.g., substance abuse, risky driving habits, and unprotected sex). Arnett suggests that risk-taking is part of an individual's "identity exploration." Young adults, those between the ages of 15 and 25, are less likely to be monitored by their parents and are unburdened by adult responsibilities; thus, they feel free to experiment with a wide range of risk behaviors, to include binge drinking and drinking and driving.

Although Arnett's (2000) and Moffitt's (1993) developmental concepts offer separate perspectives about juvenile/young adult motivation for drinking and drunk driving, they do concur on several issues. First, as juveniles move towards independence and away from parental control, parental control (social sanctions) becomes insignificant in deterring alcohol use and drunk driving in these juveniles (Corbett & Simon, 1992; Grasmick & Bursik, 1990; PCCD, 2004; Pogarsky, 2002). Second, since the motivation for drinking alcohol and drunken driving is to mimic adult behavior (Moffitt), or to seek pleasure through risky behaviors and gain experience (Arnett), juveniles will not perceive legal sanctions as a deterrent (Donohew et al., 1999; Grasmick & Bursik, 1990; Paternoster, 1989; PCCD, 2004; Pogarsky, 2002; Tibbetts, 1997).

Developmental theories predict that alcohol use by adolescence-limited offenders is deemed by juveniles to be a right of passage towards adulthood (Marks et al., 1992; Moffitt, 1993) or that alcohol use by young adults is correlated both with the thrill of risk-taking and the need to gain personal experience (Arnett, 2000; Cohn, MacFarlane, Yanez, & Imai, 1995). Though differing in their motivational aspects, both theories hypothesize that, since deviance and risk-taking are a part of normal human development, the majority of juveniles will commit some types of deviant or reckless acts, often while under the influence of alcohol. When juveniles lack direct adult supervision, often the desire to defy adult restrictions and the thrill of being together can result in illegal, dangerous, and destructive behavior (Dishion, Andrews, & Crosby, 1995; Gerrard et al., 1996).

Cognitive Functioning

The human brain is still developing when a person reaches age 20 (Nejman, 2002; Swartzwelder, 1998). Because the adolescent brain is in a developmental stage, it responds to alcohol differently than does the adult (fully developed) brain. The presence of small amounts of alcohol in the developing brain causes a chemical imbalance that affects both decision-making and memory. Decision-making and memory can be impaired in the developing brain by the alcohol equivalent to that found in one 12-ounce beer (Swartzwelder, 1998).

Recently, research has attempted to determine the long-term impact of early alcohol use on brain development. Research has shown that the earlier the onset of consuming alcohol occurs, and the more alcohol an individual consumes, especially if binge drinking, the more likely it is that the prefrontal cortex and the hippocampus will be damaged (Nejman, 2002; Swartzwelder, 1998). Nejman (2002) notes:

> Teen drinkers are susceptible to damage in two key areas of the brain, the hippocampus and the prefrontal cortex… The hippocampus is found in the brain's limbic system, which handles memory

> and learning. The prefrontal cortex, found behind a person's forehead, is important for decision-making and reasoning (p. 1).

Research also has shown that it takes less alcohol to damage a developing brain than it does an adult brain. Further, similar to the central nervous system, once the hippocampus and prefrontal cortex have been extensively damaged by alcohol abuse, they cannot be repaired since they are not self-regenerating (Nejman, 2002).

Based on this preliminary research about the effects of alcohol on the developing brain, juveniles may be limited in their abilities to make rational decisions (drinking and driving) after consuming even small amounts of alcohol. Juveniles, who abused alcohol early in their lives, may be incapable of assessing the impact of sanctions as result of damage to the prefrontal cortex and the hippocampus. The ability to assess the long-term consequences if caught drinking and driving is the foundation of deterrence theory. The inability to recognize the certainty and severity of sanctions nullifies the deterrent aspects intended by the law (Corbett & Simon, 1992; Erickson et al., 1977; Paternoster, 1989).

Synopsis of Research Findings

The Pennsylvania zero-tolerance juvenile drinking and driving law was implemented because of the failure of the minimum legal drinking age (MLDA) law to deter juveniles from drinking and subsequently driving. If the MLDA had deterred juveniles from drinking, there would have been no need for the zero-tolerance legislation. It would appear that legislators were very optimistic to assume that one deterrence-based law would succeed where another had failed.

Marginal deterrence, to include legal, social, and personal sanctions, appears to be effective in deterring a majority of juveniles from drinking and driving. The inability of marginal deterrence (at its current level) to deter a particular segment of juveniles from drinking and driving appears to be strongly supported by empirical research (Corbett & Simon, 1992; Erickson et al., 1977; Hilton, 1984; Hingson et al., 1987; Paternoster, 1989; Pogarsky, 2002; Ross et al., 1981). In two separate studies, the percentage of those juveniles who are most likely to drink and drive regardless of the punishment is estimated at between 32% and 38% (Pogarsky, 2002; Corbett & Simon, 1992, respectively).

Research has shown that those juveniles most likely to be deterred from drinking and driving by legal sanctions are the same individuals who also would have refrained from committing the offense based on the threat of personal and social sanctions (Paternoster, 1987; Pogarsky, 2002). The percentage of juveniles who can be deterred from drinking and driving may depend more on moral development, peer association, societal condemnation, and personal punishment and punishment avoidance for drinking and driving, than the threat of legal sanctions (Corbett & Simon, 1992; Erickson et al., 1977; Grasmick & Bursik, 1990; Lanza-Kaduce, 1988; Paternoster, 1989; Pogarsky, 2002; Tibbetts, 1997).

The rationale as to why legal sanctions fail to deter juveniles from committing alcohol related offenses, to include drinking and driving, is mixed. Research cites possible causes as the lack of certainty of arrest, the need for risk taking, normal adolescence development, and the impact of alcohol on brain development. Where the research does converge is about the fact that the threat of legal sanctions most often fails to deter juveniles from consuming alcohol and committing the offense of drunk driving.

Summary

Multiple studies have been conducted within numerous states about the impact of raising the legal drinking age to 21 years of age (e.g., Figlio, 1995; Hilton, 1984; Hingson et al., 1987; Muller, 1989; Ross et al., 1981; West et al., 1989), but no studies were located that specifically assessed the impact of zero-tolerance juvenile drunk driving laws, although all fifty states have enacted such legislation to remain eligible for federal highway funding. In the studies that were conducted on the impact of raising the legal drinking age to 21, the outcome measure most often used to assess the effectiveness of the law was fatality accident rates involving juvenile drunk drivers, with the law enactment date identified as the treatment.

A determination as to whether raising the legal drinking age in a state was an effective deterrent in preventing juvenile alcohol use was based on whether there was a significant, permanent change between the pre- and post-intervention trends for juvenile fatality accident rates. Because the mandatory drinking age law essentially created a new offense (possession or use of alcohol by an individual between the ages of 18 and 20), arrest rates were not used as an outcome measure to assess the impact of the law, since pre-treatment observations were not available to establish a pre-intervention trend.

For this proposed study, the zero-tolerance juvenile drunk driving law did not create a new offense, but lessened the standards (.10 mg/ml BAC to .02 mg/ml BAC) to charge a juvenile for an existing offense (drunk driving). Further, by mandating that the charge of drunk driving replace the charge of underage drinking, the legal sanctions (and arguably the social and personal repercussions) for offending were substantially increased. Theoretically, using deterrence theory as a model, the increase in the severity of sanctions should deter would-be offenders from drinking any amount of alcohol and then attempting to operate a motor vehicle.

In staying with the deterrence philosophy, an increase in the certainty, proportional severity, and/or swiftness for a particular offense should raise the marginal deterrence level for that offense, thus deterring a larger segment of the target population (juveniles) from committing the offense. Under this assumption, the use of juvenile arrest rates for drunk driving and juvenile driver alcohol related fatality accident rates will offer an accurate impact assessment of Pennsylvania's zero-tolerance juvenile drunk driving law.

One measure of the law's impact is how it affected juvenile drunk driving arrest rates. For the law to be considered effective in achieving its objective of deterring juveniles from drinking and driving, post-treatment juvenile drunk driving arrest rates ideally should decline immediately, abruptly, and permanently when the treatment is introduced, with statistically significant differences identified between pre- and post-treatment trends. A post-treatment reaction as just described would infer that juveniles were willfully complying with the law. Based on free will and rational choice, juveniles refrained from drinking and driving since the post-treatment charge of drunk driving had far greater legal sanctions associated with it than did the pre-treatment charge of underage drinking. Similarly, if there is a high correlation between juvenile fatality accident rates and juveniles who operate a motor vehicle with BAC levels under .10 mg/ml, there should be a corresponding drop in juvenile fatality accident rates.

A second measure of the law's impact is how it affected juvenile driver alcohol related fatality accidents. An argument could be made that the law has achieved its objective if after the law was enacted juvenile drunk driving arrest rates remained constant and juvenile fatality accident rates declined. Although, hypothetically, marginal deterrence is enhanced by increasing legal sanctions, by lowering the standards to charge a juvenile with drunk driving, a larger segment of the juvenile population, who do drink and drive, become more likely to be charged with drunk driving instead of underage drinking. If juvenile drunk driving arrest rates remain constant between pre-and post-treatment observations, the law could be deemed effective since the level of offending has remained constant while the pool of potential offenders has increased. The positive effect of lower juvenile fatality accident rates, coupled with the lack of an increase in juvenile drunk driving arrest rates, would be deemed an acceptable outcome.

If the legislation is not achieving its intended outcome, the reduction of juveniles using small amounts of alcohol (BAC .02 mg/ml - .09 mg/ml) and then operating a motor vehicle, post-treatment juvenile drunk driving arrest rates would immediately, abruptly, and permanently increase. Should the data indicate this effect, an assessment would be needed to determine whether the investment of criminal justice resources devoted to implementation and enforcement of this law were a worthwhile expenditure, especially if no decrease is observed in juvenile fatality accident rates.

Through the use of simple ITS designs and ARIMA modeling, an accurate assessment of the impact of Pennsylvania's zero-tolerance juvenile drunk driving law was made using both juvenile drunk driving arrest rates and juvenile fatality accident rates as outcome variables. Additional ITS designs, using other related dependent variables, were used to assess the validity of the research findings. Finally, through the use of informal, semi-structured interviews with law enforcement supervisors and an extensive review of archival data, implementation and enforcement issues were assessed to determine whether they impacted on the observed post-treatment effects of the law.

Chapter 3

Assessing Juvenile Drunk Driving Legislation

A legal impact study represents an attempt to ascertain how a particular law affects the conduct and attitudes of those individuals, groups, or other relevant units located in jurisdictions where that law is in force. By its very nature such a study involves one essential comparison; the comparison between actual behavior patterns in jurisdictions having the law in question and the behavior patterns which would have existed in those same jurisdictions had the law in question never have been enacted. Since the comparison is one in which by definition cannot actually be made, the problem for the legal impact theorist is how to estimate best what the behavior patterns would have been in a certain jurisdiction had the law in question never existed there (Lempert, 1966, p. 111).

The intent of this research was to assess the effectiveness of Pennsylvania's zero-tolerance juvenile drunk driving law in deterring juveniles (those under the age of 21) from drinking and driving. Although archival data was reviewed to identify any plausible media effects, and interviews were conducted with law enforcement supervisors regarding implementation and enforcement issues associated with this law, the primary methodology utilized was interrupted time-series (ITS) designs. ITS designs have been used previously, and successfully, to determine the impact of various types of laws and treatments (Katz, Weber, & Schaeffer, 2001; Krimmel & Mele, 1998; Reynolds et al., 2000), especially the impact of drinking age laws (Figlio, 1995; Hilton, 1984; Muller, 1989; Ross et al., 1981; West et al., 1989).

Through the employment of four ITS designs, the impact of Pennsylvania's zero-tolerance juvenile drunk driving law was assessed. The methodology used simple ITS designs to assess the impact of the law on juvenile drunk driving arrest rates and fatality vehicle accident rates resulting from juvenile drunk driving. Three more elaborate ITS designs were modeled, using dependent variables which theoretically should not be impacted by the implementation of this law, in an attempt to identify and control for threats to validity, which are plausible when using only simple ITS designs.

The use of standardized data, based on state level UCR information, enhanced both the between state and between offenses comparisons employed as part of this methodology. Further, the data was sufficient to permit 79 pre-treatment monthly observations and 89 post-treatment monthly observations for each dependent variable, thus ensuring that ample observations were present to permit the use of various statistical analysis programs. The primary analysis method used was visual analysis and ARIMA modeling.

The methods section of this paper begins with an overview of the independent and dependent variables, which were used to assess the impact of this legislation, along with the source for these data. The data source section is followed by a review of the specific ITS designs used in the research. The methods section continues with a brief discussion about ITS design analysis and a description of the possible effects a treatment, such as a new law, could create. The four ITS designs used in this study (simple, nonequivalent no-treatment control group, nonequivalent dependent variables, and switching replications) are diagramed, threats specific to each design are addressed, and anticipated treatment results are forecasted. Following the ITS design section, the general threats to validity when using ITS designs are discussed, along with the necessity for informal, semi-structured interviews with law enforcement supervisors and archival data searches to strengthen the research design. Finally, concerns about the strengths and limitations of the overall methodological design for this study are discussed.

Data and Sources

Independent Variable

One criteria for an ITS design is that it has an independent variable, which changes abruptly at a specific time (Ross, 1982). For this research, the independent variable is the change in Pennsylvania's juvenile drunk driving law. Pennsylvania's zero-tolerance juvenile drunk driving legislation was enforceable, by law enforcement agencies within the Commonwealth, on August 01, 1996 (Sen. M. J. White, personal communication, October 27, 2003). The observations surrounding this date, the impact area, becomes the primary point of focus for any changes identified in monthly observations of the dependent variables used in the various ITS models. A second criterion for an ITS design is a set of dependent variables which have been reliably measured over time and should be predicted to react sharply to the law's enactment, along with other dependent variables identified as useful in assessing the impact of the new law and controlling for threats to the research findings (Ross, 1982).

Dependent Variables

Two dependent variables used in this proposed research to assess the impact of Pennsylvania's zero-tolerance juvenile drunk driving law are Pennsylvania's juvenile drunk driving arrest rates and Pennsylvania's motor vehicle fatality rates, where the operator of the at-fault vehicle was an intoxicated juvenile. The argument has been made that motor vehicle fatality accident rates are an acceptable proxy variable for drunk driving rates (Figlio, 1995; Hilton, 1984; Hingson et al., 1987; Mueller, 1989; West et al., 1989). The belief is that motor vehicle fatality accidents have a 100% reporting rate, where many drunken driving arrests go unreported and substantially more are undetected by the police. The under-reporting of drunk driving arrests and the lack of detecting drunken drivers opens drunk driving arrest rates to enforcement and reporting biases, which are seldom found in fatality accident reporting.

To counter the argument that motor vehicle fatality accident rates are a more accurate measure of the impact of drunk driving legislation than arrest rates for drunk driving, Hingson (1993) noted that research which relies solely on motor vehicle fatality accident reporting fails to account for other laws such as mandatory seatbelt laws, which have reportedly reduced the number of motor vehicle fatality accidents. He further contends that research cannot assess the number of motor vehicle fatalities prevented by both in-vehicle safety features and external road barrier designs. Finally, he highlights that advances in emergency room procedures, first-responders decreased response times, and emergency life-flights all could decrease the number of motor vehicle fatality accidents, thus displaying a downward trend overtime, which could be mistakenly attributed to the passage of drunk driving legislation.

These two dependent variables, Pennsylvania's juvenile drunk driving arrest rates and Pennsylvania's juvenile motor vehicle fatality accident rates, would be anticipated to react sharply and immediately to the enforcement date of the zero-tolerance drunk driving legislation. Using both Pennsylvania's juvenile motor vehicle fatality accident rates, where the cause of the accident is attributed to a juvenile driver who was intoxicated, and Pennsylvania's juvenile arrest rate for drunk driving, presents a more accurate impact of Pennsylvania's zero-tolerance drunk driving law than would restricting this study to either one or the other.

The Pennsylvania State Police provided Pennsylvania's juvenile drunk driving arrest data, as well as Pennsylvania's adult drunk driving arrest data and Pennsylvania's juvenile public intoxication arrest data, which are two additional dependent variables that were used to control for threats to validity. The data was obtained from the Commonwealth's Uniformed Crime Report database (PA UCR), covering the period from January 1990 to December 2003 (79 pre-treatment monthly observations and 89 post-treatment monthly observations). This data included all arrests for these offenses recorded by the Pennsylvania State Police, as well as those from law enforcement agencies within the Commonwealth that contribute data to the PA UCR. An accurate estimate of the percentage of law enforcement agencies in Pennsylvania which contribute data to the UCR could not be obtained, but the reporting agency list has remained virtually unchanged since January 1990 (Cpl. W. J. McAreavy, personal communication, January 29, 2004), thus the monthly data, though not all inclusive, is comparable.

Ohio and Pennsylvania's Departments of Transportation provided the number of juvenile and adult motor vehicle licensed drivers registered within their respective state for each year from 1990 through 2003. Ohio and Pennsylvania's juvenile and adult drunk driving arrest rates were determined by dividing the number of arrests for the particular offense by the number of licensed drivers for each category.

Ohio and Pennsylvania's juvenile motor vehicle fatality accident data were provided by the National Highway Transportation Safety Administration's Fatality Analysis Reporting System (FARS, 2003). FARS has the capability to provide the monthly data about the number of Ohio and Pennsylvania's fatality accidents, where the cause of the accident was attributed to a juvenile driver who was operating a motor vehicle while intoxicated, for each month from January 1990 to December 2003. Again, by dividing the number of fatality accidents, where the cause of the accident is attributed to a juvenile driver who was intoxicated, by the number of licensed juvenile drivers provided the monthly fatality accident rates for each state.

The use of Ohio and Pennsylvania's monthly juvenile drunk driving arrest rates and monthly juvenile motor vehicle fatality accident rates, from January 1990 through December 2003, provided an assessment of the impact of Ohio and Pennsylvania's zero-tolerance juvenile drunk driving legislation. Although these two variables permitted statistical inferences about the impact of the legislation, they failed to control for other factors that could be contributing to any observed effect. Through the use of ITS designs with nonequivalent variables (e.g., PA adult drunk driving arrest rates and PA juvenile public intoxication rates) many of the internal threats to validity can be identified and construct validity of the effect enhanced (Shadish et al., 2002). Nonequivalent variables should not react to the treatment, but would be predicted to react similarly to the variable of interest to other plausible threats to internal and construct validity, such as general enforcement efforts, media effects, and alcohol accessibility by juveniles.

Four additional dependent variables used in this research, which are not anticipated to react to the enforcement of Pennsylvania's zero-tolerance juvenile drunk driving law, were Pennsylvania's adult drunk driving arrest rates, Pennsylvania's juvenile public intoxication arrests, as well as Ohio's juvenile drunk driving arrest rates and alcohol-related juvenile motor vehicle fatality rates. The incorporation of these dependent variables into the research permitted the addition of other ITS models. These enhanced ITS designs were intended to offer support for any inferences that changes observed between the pre- and post-treatment observations for PA juvenile drunk driving arrest rates and/or PA juvenile fatality accident rates were a result of the enactment of the law and not the cause of a third or rival variable (Shadish et al., 2002).

It was hypothesized that Pennsylvania's arrest rates for adult drunk drivers should not be impacted by the zero-tolerance juvenile drunk driving law, but would be impacted by increased enforcement efforts to deter drunk driving in general. It would be expected that if Pennsylvania's zero-tolerance juvenile drunk driving law is effective, post-treatment observations for Pennsylvania's juvenile drunk driving arrest rates should display a change in trend from pre-treatment observations. If this change in trend was due entirely to the enactment of the zero-tolerance juvenile drunk driving law (willful compliance by juveniles), no similar change in trend would be anticipated in adult drunk driving arrest rates since the new law, as drafted, should not impact them. If changes in trends were observed in both variables, there is a strong plausibility that the changes were caused by a factor other than the law, such as increased enforcement of drunk driving laws on all Pennsylvania residents regardless of age.

Similarly, the zero-tolerance juvenile drunk driving law should not impact juvenile public intoxication arrests, although both variables were anticipated to react to increased alcohol enforcement efforts and alcohol accessibility for juveniles. Since Pennsylvania raised it legal drinking age to 21 years of age prior to 1990, the observations modeled in this study was an uninterrupted trend (all post-treatment observations). If this trend is interrupted on or around the date which Pennsylvania's zero-tolerance juvenile drunk driving law was enforceable, it would indicate the strong probability of a salient third variable, which is impacting both juvenile drunk driving arrest rates and juvenile public intoxication arrests.

Although possible, it is not very plausible that the zero-tolerance juvenile drunk driving law would have a spillover effect on juvenile public intoxication arrests. Research has shown that nationally, the number of juveniles who self-report illegal alcohol use has remained virtually unchanged even though many states have enacted zero-tolerance juvenile drunk driving laws to augment their underage alcohol consumption laws (Johnston et al., 2004; Levy, 2002).

Pennsylvania's zero-tolerance juvenile drunk driving law also should not impact Ohio's juvenile drunk driving arrest rates and alcohol-related juvenile driver fatality rates. In 1994, Ohio enacted a zero-tolerance juvenile drunk driving law, which is very similar to the law enacted in Pennsylvania (Johnson, 1994). If either Ohio's juvenile drunk driving arrest rate trend or alcohol-related juvenile driver fatality rate trend are interrupted on or around the date that Pennsylvania's zero-tolerance juvenile drunk driving law was enforceable (August 01, 1996), it would weaken the causal inference attributed to the law. An interruption in Ohio's juvenile drunk driving arrest rate trend or alcohol-related juvenile driver fatality rate trend during the enactment period surrounding Pennsylvania's zero-tolerance juvenile drunk driving law would indicate that there was a national or bi-state media impact, or other historical event, which had impacted juvenile drunk driving arrest rates in both states.

Monthly data about juvenile drunk driving arrests were obtained from the Ohio State Highway Patrol. The data were not available for the time period prior to June 1993. Ohio's juvenile drunk driving arrest rates and alcohol-related juvenile driver fatality rates were chosen for contrast and comparison with Pennsylvania's data based on similarities between the states. Ohio borders Pennsylvania on the west, thus both states have very similar weather and terrain features, which could be a contributing factor in drunk driving arrest rates and fatality accident rates. Both states implemented a graduated licensing system in 1999 (OH – Jan., PA – Dec.), where juvenile drivers must obtain a learner's permit, followed by a probationary or intermediate license, and then the issuance of a full privilege license at age 18. Further, both states have a mandatory driver's education training program for drivers who request a license prior to age 18.

According to 2003 statistical data, residents of Ohio annually drive slightly more miles (13,778) than those in Pennsylvania (12,521), and Ohio has slightly more licensed drivers per 1,000 residents than does Pennsylvania, 681 and 670 respectively. Pennsylvania, though, has a slightly larger population than Ohio. In total population, Pennsylvania ranks 6th in the United States and Ohio ranks 7th. Geographically, Pennsylvania ranks 33rd in total area and Ohio ranks 34th (McGeveran, 2004). Overall, these data further confirm the similarity in the states in regards to driving related issues.

Finally, according to statistics published by the National Highway Transportation Safety Administration (FARS, 2003), between 1990 and 2003, the annual rate of fatality accidents per one million licensed drivers in Ohio (114) and Pennsylvania (109) are very similar. During this same time period, the annual rate of alcohol related fatality accidents per 100,000 licensed juvenile drivers in Ohio (8.04) and Pennsylvania (10.3) also have remained comparable. Based on the comparable juvenile drunk driving laws passed 30 months apart in both states and their associated penalties, along with parallel licensing requirements, similar populations, geographical settings, and fatality accident numbers, Ohio appeared to be an excellent match to use in a switching replication ITS design.

"The design controls most threats to internal validity, and it enhances external and construct validity" (Shadish et al., 2002, p. 192). By modeling juvenile drunk driving arrest rates between 1990 and 2003 for both Ohio and Pennsylvania, these two nonequivalent groups become control groups for each other. Since the two groups received the same treatment, but at different times (Ohio, 1994 and Pennsylvania, 1996), Pennsylvania juveniles served as a control group when Ohio juveniles received the treatment, and Ohio juveniles served as a continued treatment group when Pennsylvania (the initial control group) enacted its juvenile drunk driving legislation.

Interrupted Time-Series (ITS) Designs
$O_1\ O_2 \ldots O_{77}\ O_{78}\ O_{79}\ \ X\ \ O_{80}\ O_{81}\ O_{82}\ O_{83}\ O_{84} \ldots O_{168}$.

ITS Concept

A simple ITS design consists of multiple observations of a variable, which is interrupted by a specific, well defined treatment. For legal impact studies, the independent variable often is the date a new law is enacted, and is identified as the treatment (X). "The key here is knowing the specific point in the series at which a treatment occurred" (Shadish et al., 2002, p. 172). The dependent variable(s) are independent, equally spaced observations (O_t), most often based on similar time periods ($_t$), which occurred prior to and after the treatment. The null hypothesis is that the treatment will not impact the established pre-treatment trend (e.g., $O_1 \ldots O_{79}$). If the null hypothesis is rejected, then any change in the series could be attributed to the treatment, which for this research is the enactment of Pennsylvania's zero-tolerance juvenile drunk driving law.

This research was designed to assess the impact of Pennsylvania's zero-tolerance juvenile drunk driving law through the use of various ITS designs and qualitative methods. By modeling the pre-treatment observations, a trend is established to predict what the post-treatment observations would have most likely been had the treatment not occurred (counterfactual). The counterfactual is the projection of what would have occurred without the introduction of a treatment. "The counterfactual is a projection of the correctly modeled before series into the time periods occurring after the intervention point" (Mohr, 1988, p. 147). Since it is impossible to accurately predict what would have happened without the enactment of the law, the researcher uses pre-treatment data to establish a theoretical post-treatment pattern. The difference between what actually occurred after the law was implemented and the theoretical post-treatment pattern is then compared through regression analysis, visual analysis, and/or Autoregressive, Integrated, Moving Average (ARIMA). These methods of comparison are addressed later in the analysis section (Chapter IV).

Types of Effects

What actually occurs after a law is implemented and the theoretical post-treatment pattern can differ in numerous ways (See Appendix A: *Types of Effects*). By modeling the pre-treatment observations, monthly patterns and trends, along with seasonal changes in the observations, can be established. By knowing the exact time the treatment was introduced, changes in the established trend, if any, can be identified. Most often these changes in trend will be in the form of changes in the level (intercept) or changes in the slope, which occur near or at the treatment point (Mohr, 1988; Shadish et al., 2002). Further, multiple post-treatment observations permits the researcher to determine if the change in intercept or slope was continuous/permanent or discontinuous/temporary, as well as whether the change was immediate or delayed. Although ITS designs can capture trend changes in the dependent variable, these changes, if any, may not always be attributable to the treatment. The mere use of ITS designs does not automatically rule out threats to validity, which also could have caused a change in the trend of the dependent variable.

Internal Validity

Internal validity refers to inferences about whether one variable has a causal relationship to another (X > Y). To support this inference, it must be shown that X and Y are correlated, that X precedes Y, and that there are no other explanations for the relationship between X and Y (Akers, 2000; Paternoster & Bachman, 2001; Shadish et al., 2002). Shadish et al. (2002) identified nine factors that could mislead researchers about the causal inferences observed between variables. These nine factors are: ambiguous temporal precedence, selection, history, maturation, regression, attrition, testing, instrumentation, and additive and interactive effects of threats to internal validity (p. 55).

Lempert (1966) suggested that in using ITS designs to research the impact of a specific law, ambiguous temporal precedence, maturation, regression, attrition, and testing can be cautiously disregarded. For this type of research, the date the law is enforceable, which is clearly defined and specific, becomes the independent variable (X). Ambiguous temporal precedence is less of a threat since the enforcement date of the law is clearly defined (August 01, 1996). Pre- and post-treatment observations are defined based on the date of the observation in relation to the enforcement date of the law.

Maturation is not a plausible threat to this research, since juvenile attitudes about alcohol use have remained constant over the thirteen-year span that these data address. For maturation to become an issue in this research, juvenile attitudes towards alcohol use and drinking and driving would have to change significantly from a preceding age group. Research indicates that juvenile attitudes about alcohol use have remained relatively stable during the time frame covered by this research (Johnston et al., 2004; Levy, 2002; PCCD, 2004).

Internal validity threats based on regression artifacts and testing can be guardedly dismissed since units are not being selected based on any type of score or test. The pre- and post-treatment observations used in the various ITS designs are those monthly offenses recorded by the police. Further, by modeling the trend of the data, regression to the means is detectable. Through the use of multiple pre- and post-treatment observations, the plausibility of validity issues related to regression to the means becomes less of a threat. Finally, attrition, though a possible internal validity threat, does not appear to be a plausible threat, since the dependent variables are measured as rates based on the number of offenses for a particular crime divided by the number of licensed drivers in an age category. The use of rates of offending controls for population fluctuations, loss of driver's licenses for previous offending, and other issues which could cause attrition from Pennsylvania and Ohio's general population of juveniles and adults. The most plausible internal validity threats to an ITS design are selection, history, instrumentation, and history x selection interaction (Lempert, 1966).

The issue of selection bias is related to the police officers' discretions to arrest, and in this particular study, is closely associated with instrumentation validity. The change in the standards for establishing juvenile drunk driving (lowering the BAC level from .10 mg/ml to .02 mg/ml) may not be acceptable to law enforcement personnel, based on the stigmatization and harsh punishments associated with a conviction for drunk driving. In looking at arrest rates, these data fail to account for those officers who used their discretion to issue warnings rather than arrest juveniles who were identified as consuming trace or small amounts of alcohol. In an attempt to control for the possibility of selection effects, informal/semi-structured interviews were conducted with state law enforcement supervisors to determine their perceptions about enforcement and implementation issues related to the zero-tolerance juvenile drunk driving law.

History x selection interaction may occur as a result of law enforcement officials initially supporting enforcement of the law, and then over time, for a multitude of reasons, support for the law deteriorates causing it to lose its deterrent effect (certainty of punishment). Although juvenile arrest rates and fatality accident rates may drop sharply immediately following a law's enactment, they often return to pre-intervention levels based on the offender's perceived lack of certainty of arrest or punishment (e.g., Hilton, 1984; Hingson et al., 1987; Muller, 1989; Ross et al., 1981; West et al., 1989). The cause of this return to pre-intervention levels may be less attributable to policy failure than to policy implementation and monitoring by law enforcement officials (Dunn, 1994; Hingson et al., 1987; Ross et al., 1981).

Through the use of informal/semi-structured interviews with law enforcement supervisors an attempt was made to identify perceptions about the feasibility of enforcing Pennsylvania's zero-tolerance juvenile drunk driving law. Further, an attempt was made to determine what impact, if any, the law has had on law enforcement operations and policies. These two factors could have a significant influence on how aggressive law enforcement officers enforced the new drunk driving standards on juveniles. If enforcement of the law places an unforeseen burden on other parts of the criminal justice system, or the effort and hours expended in arresting and processing juveniles for drunk driving, based on low blood alcohol levels, were deemed as wasted man-hours, the law may receive low enforcement efforts. The attitudes law enforcement officers possess about enforcement of this law will affect arrest rates and the statistical results based on those arrest rates. To control for threats to internal validity as a result of selection bias and history, it became imperative to identify the perceptions law enforcement supervisors possess about the implementation and enforcement of Pennsylvania's zero-tolerance juvenile drunk driving law.

The most serious threat to the internal validity of an ITS design is that of history (Lempert, 1966). A researcher must attempt to determine what else, if anything, was occurring at the time of the law's enactment, which could have impacted the dependent variable(s). The use of archival information (newspaper articles from January 1995 – December 1997 that focus on informing the general public of this law) and interviews with law enforcement supervisors aided in identifying historical incidents or implementation issues, which could have impacted the observations. A second approach to control for historical threats to validity, which also was used in this research, is by modifying the simple ITS designs, used initially to assess the impact of the law on juvenile drunk driving arrest rates and juvenile fatality accident rates, to include dependent variables which are not anticipated to be impacted by this law. The use of this multiple data assessment approach, using both qualitative and quantitative data assessment techniques, offered a clearer understanding of the true impact of the law on juvenile drunk driving arrest rates and juvenile fatality traffic accident rates, while controlling for plausible threats to the validity of the research findings.

In summary, there are a myriad of possible validity threats, which could affect the results of research that uses quasi-experimental designs and secondary data obtained from official police statistics. One of the researcher's primary responsibilities becomes that of identifying which threats are most plausible or salient, and then controlling for those threats. Where control of plausible threats is not possible, the impact of the threat on the data is identified, hypothesized, and listed as a research limitation (Creswell, 1994). For this research, the identified plausible threats to validity that could impact post-treatment observation, but are unrelated to the treatment were: 1) differences in pre- and post-treatment enforcement by law enforcement officers; 2) media effects; 3) historical events; and 4) juvenile alcohol accessibility.

The use of multiple ITS designs, with additional dependent variables, along with qualitative research methods, enhanced the opportunity to assess the impact of this legislation, while controlling for the identified plausible threats to internal validity (See Table 1). Dependent variables, such as adult drunk driving arrest rates, juvenile public intoxication arrests, and Ohio's juvenile drunk driving arrest rates should not be impacted by Pennsylvania's juvenile drunk driving law. If these dependent variables do react to the treatment, the researcher is warned that there may be other plausible causes, other than the treatment, which are affecting these dependent variables (Shadish et al., 2002).

Table 1.

Plausible Threats to Validity and Methodological Control

Validity Threat	Specific Threat	Methodological Control
Statistical Conclusion	Autocorrelation Unreliability of Measures Statistical Analysis	ARIMA modeling Multiple Outcome Measures 100 + Observations per Variable
Internal	History/Media Effect History x Selection Alcohol Availability and Enforcement Interstate Issues	Archival Data Check Multiple ITS Models Multiple ITS Models Multiple ITS Models OH/PA Switching Replications
Construct	Treatment Diffusion Pre-Treatment Impact Mono-Operation Bias	Multiple Pre- & Post-Observations Archival Data Check Model Evaluation Both DUI & Fatality Accident Rates
External	Interactions of Causal Relations with Settings	Data Collected on OH & PA Juvenile Drunk Driving Arrest Rates

The addition of a qualitative component added to the research's validity. Knowing how law enforcement supervisors perceived the law's deterrent effect and their perceptions of implementation issues, assisted in explaining post-treatment trends. Archival data assisted in identifying plausible media effects, especially for the observation periods surrounding the law's enforcement date. The combined qualitative/quantitative approach offered the most effective means of eliminating the identified plausible threats to validity surrounding this research.

ITS Design Overview

An ITS design with numerous pre- and post-treatment observations "is nearly ideal for ruling out many threats to internal validity" (Shadish et al., 2002, p. 175). Six separate ITS models were used to assess the impact of Pennsylvania's zero-tolerance juvenile drunk driving law. Two of these models were simple ITS designs used to assess the impact of the law on juvenile drunk driving arrest rates and on juvenile fatality traffic accident rates involving juvenile drunk drivers. Four more elaborate ITS models were used to control for threats to validity that can occur when data are modeled in only simple ITS designs (i.e., historical threats).

A simple ITS design is defined as having one treatment group (e.g., juvenile drunk driver rates or fatality accident rates involving juvenile drunk drivers) with numerous pre- and post-treatment observations. Multiple, evenly spaced pre- and post-treatment observations are desired to permit trends in the data to be modeled. Modeling, although possible, with a small number of pre- and post-treatment observations limits the ability to detect, either visually or statistically, effects that might have been caused by a regression to mean or other seasonal/trend patterns.

ITS Model 1

Using a simple ITS design, the dependent variable was monthly observations (O_i) of Pennsylvania's juvenile drunk driving arrest rates from January 1990 through December 2003. The independent variable, or treatment (X), becomes the date of enforcement (August 01, 1996) for Pennsylvania's zero-tolerance juvenile drunk driving law.

Juvenile Drunk Driving Arrest Rates

PA Juveniles	O_1	O_2 …	O_{78}	O_{79}	X	O_{80}	O_{81} …	O_{160}

"The key here is knowing the specific point in the series at which a treatment occurred" (Shadish et al., 2002, p. 172). If the law had an impact on arrest rates, there should be a statistically significant difference in the slope and/or intercept between the pre- and post-treatment observations. "If the treatment had an impact, the causal hypothesis is that the observations after treatment will have a different slope or level from those before treatment. That is, the series should show an interruption to the prior situation at the time at which treatment was delivered" (Shadish et al., 2002, p. 172).

Using visual analysis and ARIMA modeling, an assessment was made as to the impact of Pennsylvania's zero-tolerance approach to juvenile drunk driving. Trends in arrest rates for juvenile drunk driving were modeled for both pre- and post-enactment of the zero-tolerance juvenile drunk driving law. The null hypothesis was that the enactment of the law would have no impact on the series of arrest rate observations. If the null hypothesis is rejected, then any change in the series could be cautiously attributed to the enactment of the zero-tolerance drunk driving law.

ITS Model 2

The second ITS model is identical to the first design with the exception of the dependent variable. Pennsylvania's fatality accident rates, where the cause of the accident is attributed to a juvenile driver who was intoxicated, was substituted into the design in the place of the juvenile drunk driving arrest rate variable. Hypothetically, since fatality traffic accidents have been used previously as a proxy measure for the effectiveness of drunk driving legislation, the two designs should be rather similar in the effects they display around the treatment period (Figlio, 1995; Hilton, 1984; Hingson et al., 1987; Mueller, 1989; West et al., 1989).

Monthly data about Pennsylvania's fatality accident rates was used as pre- and post-treatment observations (O_i), where the date of enforcement (August 01, 1996) for Pennsylvania's zero-tolerance juvenile drunk driving law becomes the treatment (X).

Juvenile Fatality Traffic Accident Rates

PA Juveniles	O_1	O_2	…	O_{78}	O_{79}	X	O_{80}	O_{81}	…	O_{160}

If the law had an impact on juvenile fatality accident rates involving alcohol, there should be a statistically significant difference in the trend and/or intercept between the pre- and post-treatment observations.

As previously discussed, a limitation of simple ITS designs are their susceptibility to internal validity threats, caused primarily by historical events. "With most simple interrupted time-series designs, the major threat to internal validity is history – the possibility that forces other than the treatment under investigation influenced the dependant variable at the same time at which the intervention was introduced" (Shadish et al., 2002, p. 179). To control for threats to history, additional design features were added to the simple ITS design, as discussed above and as reflected in the following ITS designs.

ITS Model 3

The simple ITS design can identify statistically significant changes in the slope or level occurring between pre-treatment and post-treatment observations. Although these changes may be statistically significant, it may be an erroneous assumption to attribute them to the treatment/independent variable, without first attempting to control for other plausible rival explanations. The third ITS model, a nonequivalent no treatment control group time series, compared PA juvenile drunk driving arrest rates with PA adult drunk driving arrest rates. The assumption was that the treatment would have no impact on PA adult drunk driving arrest rates since the law targets only juvenile offenders. If similar post-treatment changes were observed in drunk driving arrest rates for both groups, a rival explanation other than the law must be sought.

The nonequivalent no treatment control group time series places a control group, who should not be impacted by the law, with the experimental group, who should be impacted by the law. The foundation for using this design was that, as the law itself only relates to juveniles, the treatment should only impact PA juveniles. If a similar impact to that observed with PA juvenile drunk driving arrest rates was observed also with the PA adult drunk driving rates, then the threat of a third or rival variable becomes salient.

Nonequivalent No-Treatment Control Group Drunk Driving Arrest Rates

PA Juveniles	O_1	O_2	…	O_{78}	O_{79}	X	O_{80}	O_{81}	…	O_{160}
PA Adults	O_1	O_2	…	O_{78}	O_{79}		O_{80}	O_{81}	…	O_{160}

The zero-tolerance alcohol law enacted in Pennsylvania was designed to reduce the number of juvenile drunk driving incidents, which were measured here through arrest rates and fatalities. Using adults, as a control group, helped provide a more accurate assessment of the law's impact.

For this model, it was predicted that the treatment should have no impact on adult drunk driving arrest rates, but should impact juvenile drunk driving arrest rates. If after the treatment, juvenile drunk driving arrest rates decline and the trend in adult drunk driving arrest rates remains unaffected, support for the deterrence effects of the law become more plausible. Attributing a deterrent effect of the law becomes questionable if the treatment has a similar impact on both juvenile and adult drunk driving arrest rates.

The nonequivalent no treatment control group time series design, while controlling for enforcement affects, did not eliminate validity threats which may be inherent only to juveniles. Additional ITS designs were necessary to control for historical effects which may influence only juveniles, such as stricter enforcement of alcohol sales, targeting of juvenile offenders who use alcohol, or an unexplained reduction in alcohol consumption by juveniles. The final two ITS designs (nonequivalent dependent variable and switching replications) were intended to control for other historical events at the state and national level, which may affect only juveniles.

ITS Model 4

The fourth ITS model used in this study incorporated the use of a nonequivalent dependent variable design to control for threats to internal and construct validity. The variable of interest (Pennsylvania's juvenile drunk driving arrests) was compared to another related dependent variable (Pennsylvania's juvenile alcohol arrests, other than drunk driving). A key component of this relationship between variables was that the treatment should be predicted to have no effect on the nonequivalent dependent variable. Further, the nonequivalent dependent variable must be conceptually related to the primary dependent variable so it was predicted to react to internal and construct validity threats similar to the predicted reaction of the primary dependent variable (Shadish et al., 2002).

Nonequivalent Dependent Variables

PA Juveniles Drunk Driving Arrests	O_1	O_2 …	O_{78}	O_{79}	X	O_{80}	O_{81}	…	O_{160}
PA Juveniles Drunkenness Arrests	O_1	O_2 …	O_{78}	O_{79}		O_{80}	O_{81}	…	O_{160}

Shadish et al. (2002) explain:

> The plausibility of many threats to internal validity in time series can be examined and the construct validity of the effect enhanced by collecting time-series data for a dependent variable that the treatment should affect and for a nonequivalent dependent variable that a treatment should not affect but that would respond in the same way as the primary dependent variable to a pertinent validity threat. The two variables must be conceptually related (p. 184).

The intent of Pennsylvania Statute 75 Pa. C. S. 3718 was to reduce juvenile drunk driving incidents and fatality accidents. The law was not designed to impact on other types of juvenile alcohol related incidents, such as public intoxication and drunk and disorderly conduct. Using a nonequivalent dependent ITS design, data analysis assessed both possible displacement effects of the law and controlled for threats to internal validity. A rival explanation other than the treatment should be sought if both variables react similarly to the treatment (Shadish et al., 2002).

For example, if both juvenile drunk driving arrests and juvenile public intoxication arrests increase immediately after the law was enacted, the observed effect may be attributed more to enforcement of existing alcohol laws than to the enactment of the new law. Inversely, if juvenile drunk driving arrests and juvenile public intoxication arrests both decrease immediately after the law was enacted, the observed effect may be attributed more to the inability of juveniles to obtain alcohol than to the enactment of the law. Ideally, since Pennsylvania's zero-tolerance juvenile drunk driving law addresses only juvenile alcohol use while operating a motor vehicle, juvenile public intoxication arrests should not react to the passage of the law.

ITS Model 5

The fifth and final ITS design used in this study was that of switching replications. A switching replications ITS design compares two nonequivalent groups (i.e., Ohio's and Pennsylvania's juvenile drunk driving arrest rates or Ohio's and Pennsylvania's juvenile driver alcohol-related fatality rates), with each receiving the same treatment, but at different times. One group initially received the treatment (Ohio's juveniles), while the second (Pennsylvania's juveniles) acted as a control. At a later time period, the second group received the identical treatment, causing the first group to serve as a continued treatment control (Shadish et al., 2002) noted,

> The design controls most threats to internal validity, and it enhances external and construct validity. External validity is enhanced because an effect can

be demonstrated with two populations at two different moments in history, sometimes in two settings (p. 192).

Switching Replications
Juvenile Drunk Driving Arrest Rates

Ohio Juveniles	O_1 O_2 ...O_{52}	X	O_{53} ... O_{79}		O_{80}...O_{160}
PA Juveniles	O_1 O_2 ...O_{52}		O_{53} ... O_{79}	X	O_{80}...O_{160}

Using nonequivalent groups, each receiving the same treatment, but at different times, offered numerous advantages over a simple ITS design. Observations were taken for both groups prior to the first group, Ohio juveniles, receiving the treatment. It was hypothesized that the trends in the juvenile drunk driving arrest rates and juvenile driver alcohol-related fatality accidents between the two states would remain relatively consistent until observation #53 (May 04, 1994), at which time Ohio enacted its zero-tolerance juvenile drunk driving law (Johnson, 1994). Starting at observation #53, a change in the dependent variable was anticipated for Ohio, but not for Pennsylvania, which continued to operate under the less severe drunk driving standard of .10 mg/ml BAC for both adults and juveniles.

When the treatment was initiated in Pennsylvania (August 01, 1996), the Ohio juveniles served as a continued treatment control group. Since the treatment was previously imposed on Ohio juveniles, it was predicted that the trend in Ohio's post-treatment juvenile drunk driving arrest rates or juvenile alcohol-related fatality accident rates would remain relatively steady, having had 30 months to stabilize, while Pennsylvania's juvenile drunk driving arrest rates or juvenile alcohol-related fatality accident rates would react to the newly imposed treatment.

The uniqueness of this design makes it difficult for a single historical threat to explain variations between the groups since the treatments occurred 30 months apart (Shadish et al., 2002). If Ohio's juvenile drunk driving rates react to the enactment of Pennsylvania's zero-tolerance juvenile drunk driving law, there would appear to be a third variable which impacted juvenile drunk driving arrest rates in both states. The plausible presence of a third variable would question the validity of any cause and effect relationship observed between the enactment of the law and the reaction of Pennsylvania's juvenile drunk driving arrest rates.

There remains the possibility in this design for threats to internal validity. Selection history (unique local history that is different for both groups but has similar effects) and selection-instrumentation (the two groups fail to maintain the same trends prior to observation #53) are both concerns when using switching replications in an ITS design with non-equivalent groups (Shadish et al., 2002). Although these threats were possible, they did not appear plausible in that, since 1990, the two states were comparable in key variables such as juvenile drunk driving arrests, traffic accidents, and fatality traffic accidents involving alcohol (McGeveran, 2004; NHTSA, 2003b).

Qualitative Data

Informal, Semi-structured Interviews

Quantitative data provided information about the effects of the treatment on the dependent variables, but could not provide information about implementation issues surrounding enforcement of the law, and equally important, about any unintended consequences of the law, both of which could impact the quantitative data. Informal, semi-structured interviews were conducted with law enforcement supervisors who have knowledge of issues which may have impacted the implementation or enforcement of Pennsylvania's zero-tolerance juvenile drunk driving law. These interviews were designed to gather data relevant to various threats to making valid inferences about the impact of the law (See Table 1, for specific threats).

The use of the informal, semi-structured interview technique permitted the interviewees more latitude to express their observations and ideas. This technique permitted the interviewees the opportunity to expound on their description of events, which offered a better insight into the areas of emphasis identified by the interviewer (Esterberg, 2002). The areas of emphasis assessed during these interviews, pertaining to the zero-tolerance juvenile drunk driving law, were the perceived degrees of compliance by officers, the discovery of unintended consequences of the law, implementation obstacles and constraints, and any reasons for enforcement departure.

Obtaining information about these areas, which pertain to policy implementation and monitoring, was imperative for policy evaluation and assessment (Dunn, 1994). Failure to obtain information about implementation and enforcement issues related to the juvenile zero-tolerance drunk driving law could lead to inaccurate interpretations of the quantitative data, especially for observations located in the immediate proximity of the impact area (August 01, 1996). For example, if the quantitative data indicated a delayed, but gradual increase in arrest rates, law enforcement interviews stating that there was a lack of funding at the beginning of the enforcement period would assist in explaining the trend in the quantitative data. West et al. (1989) note, "that to understand the full range of effects of the intervention, the inclusion of qualitative information often can be an important aid in the interpretation of the quantitative design" (p. 1218).

In this study, multiple state-level law enforcement supervisors were contacted to obtain their perceptions about inter-departmental issues, which may have impacted the implementation and/or enforcement of Pennsylvania's zero-tolerance juvenile drunk driving law. Although all those contacted willingly offered their insight about current implementation and enforcement issues, they often lacked the historical knowledge to recall implementation and enforcement issues when the law was enacted.

Three supervisors were knowledgeable enough with the topic to recall the implementation of the law. The number of interviewees was not adjusted upward, since the responses of these three supervisors were in agreement about implementation issues and supported the information obtained from other supervisors who lacked implementation knowledge, but offered insight about current enforcement issues. Although only three law enforcement officers were in supervisory roles when the law was implemented, all of the law enforcement supervisors were asked to respond to the following questions: 1) From your perspective, how effective has the juvenile zero-tolerance drunk driving law been in deterring juveniles from drinking and driving? 2) From your position as a supervisor, what types of obstacles, constraints, or community/political pressure have been identified regarding issues with implementing and enforcing this particular law? 3) What problems, if any, have your officers had with implementing or enforcing this particular law? 4) What changes, if any, were made within your department as a result of the enactment of this law? 5) To what extent do you think state law enforcement has been able to successfully implement the law? 6) Overall, do you believe this law has been effective in achieving the goal of deterring juveniles from drinking and driving?

A myriad of issues involving the laws implementation or enforcement could have occurred that may have affected the quantitative data. Failure to address implementation and enforcement issues could cause a misinterpretation of the quantitative findings. For example, if law enforcement personnel were confronted with various obstacles or constraints which delayed the enforcement of the law (i.e., manpower shortage or funding issues), the post-treatment arrest rates would reflect this delay, giving the post-treatment observations a lagged effect. In contrast, if there was strong community/political pressure to enforce this law, juvenile drunk driving arrest rates may increase significantly after the enforcement date, but this increase would be more attributable to enforcement efforts than to an increase in juvenile drunk driving. Without this qualitative component, issues affecting implementation and enforcement, which directly impact the quantitative data, would go undetected.

Thus, the primary intent of these informal, semi-structured interviews with law enforcement supervisors was to help control for various threats to validity, which could cause a misinterpretation of the quantitative findings. These interviews enhanced statistical conclusion validity by controlling for issues involving unreliability of treatment (e.g., only partial implementation of treatment or treatment implemented differently in various locations across the Commonwealth). Further, the qualitative data enhanced internal validity by offering insight about specific law enforcement issues (e.g., selection bias, lack/loss of support for the law, implementation problems). Finally, the qualitative data assisted in controlling for plausible threats to construct validity that were related to treatment diffusion or pre-treatment impact.

Coordination and Interview Administration

A telephone call was placed to each selected law enforcement supervisor to obtain his or her permission to be interviewed, starting with the Commandant of the Pennsylvania State Police (PSP). The PSP Commandant was requested to participate, and his permission was requested to contact his troop commanders for their participation. After permission was granted, select supervisors were contacted by telephone to solicit their support to be interviewed.

During the initial telephone contact, law enforcement supervisors were briefed about the research and were asked to participate. Additionally, permission to tape record the interview was solicited. The law enforcement supervisors were assured that although anonymity could not be provided, confidentiality would be maintained, with only the researcher and the dissertation committee having access to the interviews. Further, through the use of a master roster, even the dissertation committee would not have access to which interviews came from which law enforcement supervisor. Finally, the interviewees were guaranteed that no direct quotes would be attributed to any supervisor, without their written consent.

Interview appointments were made with the law enforcement supervisors who volunteered to participate. A Letter of Introduction and a copy of the Informed Consent were forwarded to the PSP legal department and to each law enforcement supervisor who agreed to be interviewed, which provided information about the proposed research and why the interviews were an integral part of the research. The primary researcher conducted all interviews to ensure reliability. Interviews were conducted at a time selected by the interviewees. Every attempt was made to have the interview conducted in their offices during normal duty hours. Due to time constraints, all the interviewees requested the interview be completed over the telephone.

Prior to any interview starting, the interviewees were provided a copy of the informed consent form. The primary researcher read the consent form verbatim and ensured that the interviewee understood the content of the form. All law enforcement supervisors who were contacted agreed to participate, but many had insufficient knowledge of the law's implementation to respond to several of the questions. Prior to the interview, each interviewee was reminded that s/he could terminate the interview at any time. Since the interviewees were all senior law enforcement supervisors, they were familiar with informed consent policies; thus, no identified problems evolved with their understanding the consent form.

The interviews began with an introduction of the research and the first interview question (From a law enforcement perspective, how effective has the juvenile zero-tolerance drunk driving law been in deterring juveniles from drinking and driving?). The interviewee was permitted to respond to the research questions and elaborate about areas s/he believed important to understanding various aspects, which could impact the implementation and/or enforcement of the law. The interviews closed with the interviewer thanking the interviewee for participating and taking the time to offer her/his insight about the enforcement and implementation issues surrounding this particular law. Based on the information obtained from the initial interviews, no follow-up interviews were conducted. Plausible threats to the quantitative data, based on implementation and enforcement issues identified in the qualitative data, are addressed in Chapter 5.

Human Subject Protection

For this research, human subjects were interviewed in their professional capacity as law enforcement supervisors for their perceptions of implementation and enforcement issues related to Pennsylvania's zero-tolerance juvenile drunk driving laws. All participants were senior law enforcement supervisors within the Commonwealth of Pennsylvania, who voluntarily agreed to participate in the research. The reason for the research was clearly described to each of the selected supervisors. The supervisors were provided a copy of the informed consent form and were thoroughly briefed about its content prior to being interviewed.

The consent form clearly highlighted that participation was voluntary and that the interviewee could stop the interview at any time. The consent form elaborated on why the interviews were necessary, and how the researcher would use and safeguard the information obtained. Further, the interviewees were assured that their identities would remain confidential, with only the researcher and the dissertation chair having the ability to identify which interviews were given by a particular interviewee. Finally, the interviewees were assured that no direct quotes would be attributed to specific individuals and their names and/or duty positions would not appear in the final research.

Archival Data

Archival data on Pennsylvania's zero-tolerance drunk driving law was obtained from the Pennsylvania Liquor

Control Board, internet search engines, and information searches of daily newspapers from across the state. Newspaper article searches focused on any information published about Pennsylvania's zero-tolerance drunk driving law, with a primary focus on the dates surrounding its passage (July 02, 1996), its enforcement date (August 01, 1996), and any period where a trend in the data appears unexplained by statistical means or the informal, unstructured interviews with law enforcement personnel.

The retrieval of archival data was an attempt to control for various threats to validity. If media reporting about the new law caused arrest rates to decline prior to the law's enactment date, there could be a historical threat to internal validity. Media hype about the new law could have actually lowered arrest rates prior to the law taking effect. After the media hype, if arrest rates returned to the pre-treatment levels, the law would appear as if it actually increased arrest rates. Also, to eliminate a rival third variable, if the law was enacted along with a large expenditure for media publicity, knowing how the arrest rates reacted after the media campaign was discontinued would add validity to the research findings.

Strengths and Limitations

Strengths

The primary strength of this legal impact assessment was the use of two outcome measures. The use of juvenile drunk driving arrest rates, as an outcome measure, was the key difference between this research and earlier research about the impact of legislation designed to control juvenile alcohol use. In focusing only on juvenile fatality accident rates as the outcome variable to determine the effectiveness of legislation, previous research has failed to capture the full impact of the legislation.

A second strength of this research was the use of four ITS designs, and other research methods, to control for validity threats. The multiple ITS designs measured the full impact of the law on several different dependent variables. The assessment of the law's impact on multiple dependent variables eliminated many validity threats not addressed in previous drunk driving research. Threats to statistical conclusion validity remained a concern since statistical inferences were based on archival data, although this did not limit the number of observations necessary to accurately model the ITS designs. To lessen this concern, data analysis assistance was obtained through the Indiana University of Pennsylvania Mathematics Department.

Another design strength was the use of qualitative methods in an attempt to explain anomalies in the data. By interviewing law enforcement supervisors, this design offered the ability to distinguish the written law from that which is actually being enforced. To fully understand the data, it was necessary to interview law enforcement supervisors to determine their perception of implementation and enforcement issues, which may have affected the enforcement of this particular law.

Limitations

Although Pennsylvania's monthly drunk driving statistics and alcohol related incidents were reported according to PA UCR definitions and the data are standardized across jurisdictions, a limitation of the data was that not all police departments within Pennsylvania participate in UCR reporting, and Ohio has no central crime reporting procedures. This limitation should be of minimal impact, however, since those law enforcement agencies, which do report UCR data, report consistently.

This study's primary limitation (although unavoidable) was its dependence on secondary data. Although the uniformity of recording the data is one of this research's strengths, the failure of all law enforcement agencies within the state to report their statistics to the PA UCR or the Ohio Department of Public Safety leaves numerous incidents not in the data set, which were known to the police.

An additional concern with using secondary data was that the figures are subject to variation in police reporting and record keeping (Mosher, Miethe, & Phillips, 2002). Based on institutional and/or political pressure, funding needs, or a host of other possibilities, law enforcement agencies may under or over report statistics to highlight a particular need or cause. Further, officers may charge individuals with lesser offenses, such as reckless driving, in lieu of drunk driving, which would affect the secondary data. Although both of these issues could affect all the realms of validity pertaining to this study, given the central questions, this study was dependant on longitudinal data to establish trends in crime. Also, this is an issue only if it produces a systematic bias.

A final limitation of this study was the lack of previous research about the impact of zero-tolerance juvenile drunk driving laws. Since 1987, multiple studies have been conducted about the impact of increasing the drinking age (NMDA) to 21 years old (Figlio, 1995; Hilton, 1984; Muller, 1989; Ross et al., 1981; West et al., 1989), but no study was found which tested the impact of zero-tolerance juvenile drunk driving laws. Although this study was modeled after those, which did test the effect of laws that increased the drinking age, there was little research available to guide this study on how to accurately assess the impact of zero-tolerance juvenile drunk driving laws.

Chapter 4

Reducing Crime or Increasing Criminality

For this research, both quantitative and qualitative data were analyzed to assess the impact of Pennsylvania's zero-tolerance juvenile drunk driving law. The quantitative component used statistical techniques to assess the intervention impact on multiple outcome measures, to include the impact of Ohio's zero-tolerance juvenile drunk driving law. The themes identified in the qualitative data assisted in controlling for validity threats to inferences made about the law's impact based on the statistical analyses.

This chapter begins with a discussion about the strengths and weaknesses of various analysis methods which can be applied to time-series data. This section is followed by a brief description of how each ITS model was identified, estimated, and diagnosed. The chapter concludes with a description of how the qualitative data were analyzed and the importance of assessing multiple outcome measures to obtain a more comprehensive evaluation of the law's impact.

Interrupted Time-Series Design Analysis

Analysis Method

The three preferred methods of characterizing changes in an ITS design are: 1) visual inspection; 2) regression analysis; and, 3) ARIMA - autoregressive (AR), integrated (I), moving average (MA) models. Each method of characterizing changes has its own strengths and weaknesses (Mohr, 1988). For this study, ARIMA modeling was the primary means used to analyze the interrupted time-series data. Based on the expected autocorrelation in the data, ARIMA modeling was deemed more appropriate than other regression techniques to accurately interpret the changes between pre- and post-intervention observations.

Visual analysis of data sequence plots remains important since it is the primary means of identifying the starting point for ARIMA modeling, as well as offering an initial indication of the intervention's impact. Quantitative changes can be read from the graphs, if the time-series is well behaved and void of white noise (random error), which provide similar statistical results to those provided by OLS or ARIMA. "By visual inspection, one usually (not always) obtains quite an immediate and strong impression of trend just by noting whether the series seems flat or moves generally up or down over time" (Mohr, 1988, p. 154).

Regression analysis is another means of analyzing ITS data. Although regression formulas for ITS analysis exist, researchers are cautioned about their effectiveness (McDowall, McCleary, Meidinger, & Hay, 1980; Mohr, 1988; Ostrom, 1990; Shadish et al., 2002). A key difference between time series data and data used in causal comparison or other quasi-experimental research models is the plausible presence of autocorrelation within the error terms. The importance of the discussion about the disturbance or error term (u_t) cannot be overemphasized.

A critical assumption of Ordinary Least Squares (OLS) regression is that the error terms for various observations are uncorrelated (Lewis-Beck, 1980; Mohr, 1988; Shadish et al., 2002). In using OLS regression for interpreting interrupted time-series analysis, this assumption cannot be maintained. Errors at observation # 2 have a high probability of being correlated with errors at observation # 1 and # 3. Further, the error correlation could extend beyond the immediate adjoining observations (McDowall et al., 1980). Failure to control for autocorrelation could inflate the common *t* statistic by as much as 400 percent (McDowall et al., 1980; Ostrom, 1990). Since autocorrelation was present in the data, OLS was not used to assist in analyzing the data. An acceptable solution for addressing the problem of autocorrelation was the use of ARIMA modeling.

ARIMA modeling is similar to regression analysis in that it attempts to establish trends and eliminate systematic error (Mohr, 1988). Where regression analysis depends on additional independent variables to account for error, ARIMA employs the disturbance term itself as an independent variable. The concept surrounding ARIMA modeling is that a random shock (a_t) is processed through a series of filters (p, d, q), which control for autoregression (p), differencing (d), and moving average (q), and exits the filters as a time-series observation (Y_t) (McDowall et al., 1980). Further, seasonality can be controlled for by using ARIMA (p, d, q)(P, D, Q) models, where the random shock is run through additional filters, which control for seasonal autoregression (P), seasonal differencing (D), and seasonal moving average (Q). The appropriate ARIMA model is identified from the autocorrelation functions (ACF) and partial autocorrelation functions (PACF) obtained from the time-series observations.

The need for numerous pre- and post-intervention observations becomes apparent for ARIMA modeling. To accurately control for autocorrelation, sufficient observations are necessary to establish an accurate pattern of systematic error. In more complex models, requiring multiple seasonal differences, twelve observations are lost for each time the data is differenced. Thus, the recommended minimum number of observations is 100, with fairly equal amounts on both sides of the intervention point. In the current data, with the exception of the Ohio juvenile drunk driving arrest data, each of the other variables have approximately 80 observation points on each side of the intervention. The Ohio juvenile drunk driving arrest data has sufficient post-intervention observations, but only 38 pre-intervention observations. Although SPSS Trends has the capacity to model and generate missing data, this was not necessary since the ARIMA model identified for the Ohio data was a simple model, with few pre-intervention observations lost in accurately identifying an adequate ARIMA model.

ARIMA and ITS Analysis

Concept

Using the formula $Y_t = N_t + I_t$, the time-series (Y_t) is composed of a noise component (N_t) and an intervention component (I_t). The noise component includes trends in the data, seasonality, and random error, all of which could impact the statistical conclusion validity of the research findings if disregarded (McDowall et al., 1980). Further, within the random error is autocorrelation. The basic idea behind ARIMA modeling is to first identify autocorrelation within the data and then to isolate the autocorrelation by treating it as an independent variable. Through the use of ARIMA modeling, the noise term can be modeled, accounting for all three types of noise (McDowall et al.). "Once these sources of variance have been modeled, the impact of an intervention can be tested and measured" (McDowall, et al., 1980, p. 14).

Describing Post-Intervention Effects

ITS analysis is a description of the difference between reality and the counterfactual. In simpler terms, it is the difference between what really happened after an intervention and what would have been projected to happen had the intervention not occurred. The projection of what did not occur (counterfactual) is based on the pattern identified by the pre-intervention data (Mohr, 1988).

The modeling of numerous pre-intervention observations permits the establishment of a pattern or trend in the data. The two primary indicators of an intervention effect are a change in the slope or a change in the level. A comparison of the pre- and post-intervention slopes can be conducted visually and/or statistically to determine if the intervention caused any change. Ideally, changes between the pre- and post-intervention slopes will occur at the intervention point. For this study, that point is the date when the Pennsylvania juvenile drunk driving law became enforceable (August 01, 1996).

Discontinuity at the intervention point is termed "a change in the level or intercept" (Shadish et al., 2002, p. 173). Discontinuity in an ITS design is indicated by a break in the continuity of the established pre-intervention trend, at or near the time period where the intervention was introduced. The discontinuity causes the pre-intervention data and post-intervention data to have different y-intercepts.

A change in slope is indicated by an increase or decrease in the post-intervention slope, when compared to the pre-intervention slope. In simpler terms, the predicted value of "Y" ($\hat{Y}$) for any post-intervention observation is significantly different than what would have been predicted based on the pre-intervention slope. If the post-intervention observations for the true value of Y are significantly different than the predicted counterfactual, a causal inference can be made that the change in slope was a result of the intervention. The closer these changes occur to the intervention point, the more plausible it is that the change is attributable to the intervention (Shadish et al., 2002).

In reporting changes in slopes, levels, or both, it also becomes necessary to describe the characteristics of the change. The three relevant areas for describing the impact of an intervention on the slope and level are: 1) permanence or duration; 2) immediacy; and, 3) onset (McDowall et al., 1980; Mohr, 1988; Shadish et al., 2002).

The duration of the intervention effect is most often expressed as permanent or temporary. Through the use of numerous post-intervention observations, it can be determined if the intervention impact permanently adopted the new slope or level or if the intervention impact slowly deteriorated over time, returning to pre-intervention trends.

The immediacy of the intervention effect is described in terms of immediate or delayed. An immediate intervention effect occurs at the point where the intervention was introduced. A delayed intervention effect is identified as a change in the slope that occurs not at the intervention introduction point, but at a point later in the time series.

The further the effect occurs from the intervention introduction point, the greater the threat of historical validity, in that causes other than the intervention may have initiated the slope change.

Where the immediacy of the intervention effect describes when the intervention had an impact, the onset describes the intervention impact severity. The onset of the intervention effect is defined as abrupt (also referred to as a sharp discontinuity) or gradual. An abrupt onset is characterized by a sharp discontinuity within the established trend, where a gradual onset is identified by a slow moving increase or decrease in the established trend. The intervention onset is related to intervention immediacy in that where the onset occurs, defines the immediacy. (See Appendix A, Figures A1 - A7 for examples of various intervention effects).

Model Construction

Identification. ARIMA modeling consists of three distinct phases, identification, estimation, and diagnosis (SPSS Trends 10.0). The first phase, identification, is based on a visual inspection of the plotted observations and the ACF and PACF of the actual observations. Sequence plots and graphs of the ACF and PACF indicate whether the data are stationary. If the time-series is not stationary, it must be differenced (d). After obtaining a stationary series, the autoregression (p) and moving average (q) components of the model can be identified using the ACF and PACF for the error term (residual) of the differenced series.

As a rule of thumb, AR (p) processes have exponentially declining values of the ACF. In the PACF, the number of spikes outside the confidence interval indicates the starting point for AR model identification. If only the first spike was outside the PACF confidence interval, it would suggest an AR (1) process. If the first two spikes were outside the PACF confidence interval, it would suggest an AR (2) process, and so on. Usually, social science time series data does not exceed an AR (2) or MA (2) process (SPSS Trends 10.0).

For an MA (q) process, the number of spikes outside the confidence interval in the ACF indicates the starting point for model identification. If only the first spike was outside the ACF confidence interval, it would suggest a MA (1) process. If the first two spikes were outside the ACF confidence interval, it would suggest a MA (2) process, and so on. Further, MA (q) processes have exponentially declining values of the PACF (SPSS Trends 10.0).

Estimation. Using SPSS *Trends*, the tentative model is calculated and evaluated using maximum-likelihood coefficients. SPSS generates five new variables based on the tentative ARIMA model. The new variables (predicted value, residuals, upper and lower confidence intervals, and standard error of fit) are used to diagnose the model.

Diagnosis. The ACF and PACF graphs of the residuals from the tentative model should be within the upper and lower confidence limits preset by the model. Although one or two spikes may protrude outside these limits, if the protruding spikes are within the first few observations, the model is probably misspecified (SPSS Trends 10.0). If two or more models display acceptable ACFs and PACFs, additional goodness-of-fit measures are offered in the SPSS display (Akaike Information Criterion or AIC, Schwarz Bayesian or SBC, Log likelihood, Box-Ljung *Q* statistic, and t-values for each p and q parameter entered into the model) to determine which is the best model. If a model is over-specified, the *t* value will indicate that the parameter is insignificant and should be removed from the model. If a model is under specified, the residual ACFs and PACFs will remain outside the prescribed confidence limits (SPSS Trends 10.0).

Finally, when assessing ARIMA models it is important to ensure that for the AR process, ϕ remains within the bounds of stationarity and for the MA process, θ remains within the bounds of invertibility (McDowall et al., 1980). In brief, the values of ϕ_1 and θ_1 are bounded in that $-1 < \phi_1 < 1$ and $-1 < \theta_1 < 1$. ARIMA models that display unstandardized coefficients for AR_1 and MA_1 that are outside these boundaries are improperly specified.

Data Analysis

ARIMA Models

Independent sample t tests. Using the date the law was enforceable, an independent sample *t* test was conducted for each variable of interest. The independent sample *t* test was used to determine if the mean value for a particular variable was significantly different between pre- and post-intervention observations.

Model 1 – Pennsylvania Juvenile Drunk Driving Arrest Rates. Using model one as an example, a step by step process for ARIMA modeling is discussed. Evaluations of subsequent models omit elaboration about model identification, estimation, and diagnosis, and focus on the statistical analysis for that particular model. Appendix C contains sequence plots for all models using fatality accident data.

Figure 1 (below) displays a sequence plot of Pennsylvania's juvenile drunk driving arrest rates per 100,000 licensed juvenile drivers. The vertical line indicates the point where Pennsylvania's zero-tolerance juvenile drunk driving law became enforceable (August 1, 1996). The horizontal line indicates the mean of the entire series.

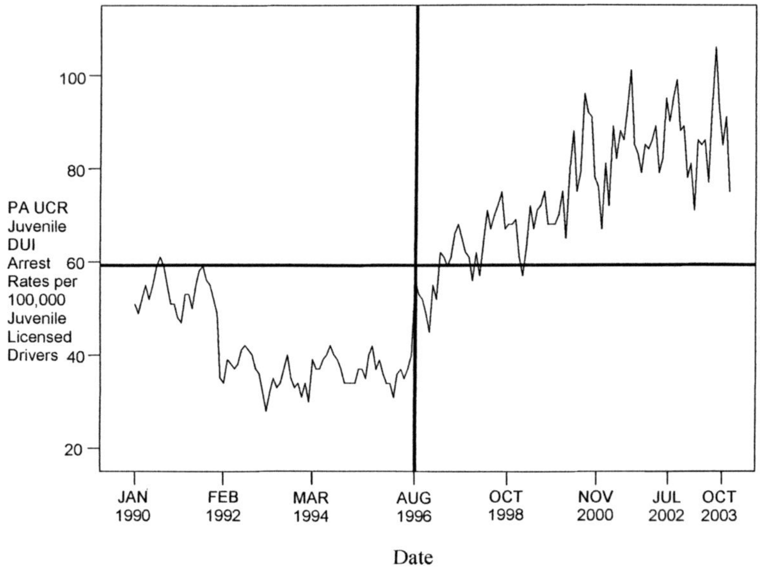

Figure 1.
Sequence plot of Pennsylvania monthly juvenile drunk driving arrest rates.

Figure 1 indicates the presence of a non-stochastic process. A visual inspection of sequence plot shows that from January 1990 through most of 1991, the monthly arrest rates were moving above and below a common mean value. Starting in late 1991 through early 1992 there was an abrupt downward trend in arrest rates, which leveled off in late 1992, but this discontinuity caused a change in the Y intercept, which was maintained until the new law was enforceable in August 1996. At the point where the zero-tolerance juvenile drunk driving law became enforceable, an immediate, gradual upward trend is observed in arrest rates. The upward trend continued through March 2000, where it again appears a new Y intercept was established throughout the remaining observations.

Further, Figure 1 suggests the presence of seasonality. Annually, August has the highest arrest rates, followed by July, September and October. Similarly, February has the lowest arrest rates, followed by December, January, and May. A six-month seasonal pattern holds true for only August and February, but a 12 month seasonal pattern appears valid throughout the observations. In other words, the value of a current observation (Y_t) is based partially on the observation that occurred 12 months previously (t_{-12}). ARIMA modeling was developed to address autocorrelation issues within a stochastic process. Figure 1 indicates that Pennsylvania juvenile drunk driving arrests are not a stochastic process, so the observations must be differenced, to include a seasonal differencing component $(0, 1, 0)(0, 1, 0)_{12}$, as depicted in Figure 2 (below).

Figure 2 indicates that the differenced data does not drift or display trends, instead, each observation moves noisily (random shock) around the mean (0). Using an ARIMA $(0, 1, 0)(0, 1, 0)_{12}$ model, the series has become a stochastic process, but the values of each random shock could be dependent on autoregressive (AR) or moving average (MA) components correlated with preceding observations. To evaluate this possibility, the ACF and PACF for the error term (residual) of the differenced series must be evaluated (Figures 3 and 4, respectively).

Figure 3 and 4 (below) indicate that the ACF is not exponentially declining, but the PACF is until lag 11. The ACF and PACF suggest a MA(q) process.

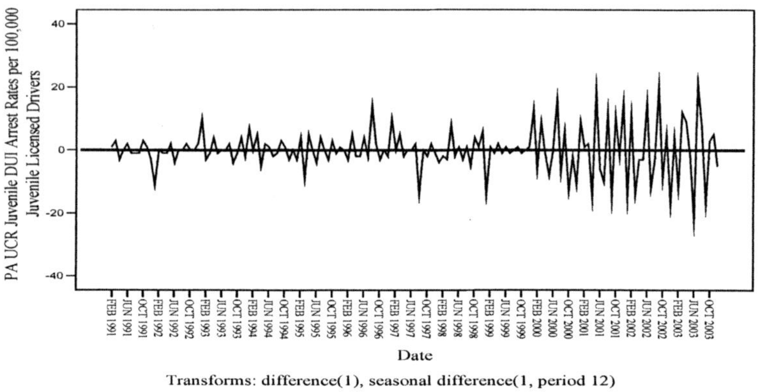

Figure 2.
Sequence plot of Pennsylvania's monthly juvenile drunk driving arrest rates ARIMA $(0, 1, 0)(0, 1, 0)_{12}$.

Figure 3 displays that several of the ACF lags are outside the model's designated confidence interval. The single spikes outside the confidence interval at lag 1 and lag 13 suggest an MA_1 process with a seasonal MA_1 (SMA_1). The MA prediction is further supported by the exponentially declining values in the PACF. Figures 3 and 4 suggest that an ARIMA $(0, 1, 1)(0, 1, 1)_{12}$ should be the starting point for identifying the appropriate ARIMA model. Figures 5 and 6 (below) represent the ACF and PACF error terms (residuals) for the ARIMA $(0, 1, 1)(0, 1, 1)_{12}$ model without a constant parameter included in the model.

The addition of the MA_1 and SMA_1 components to the differenced model confined the ACF and the PACF within the model's confidence interval. The addition of the MA_1 and SMA_1 components caused the constant parameter to become insignificant for this model (.059, $p > .261$), so this parameter was dropped from the model.

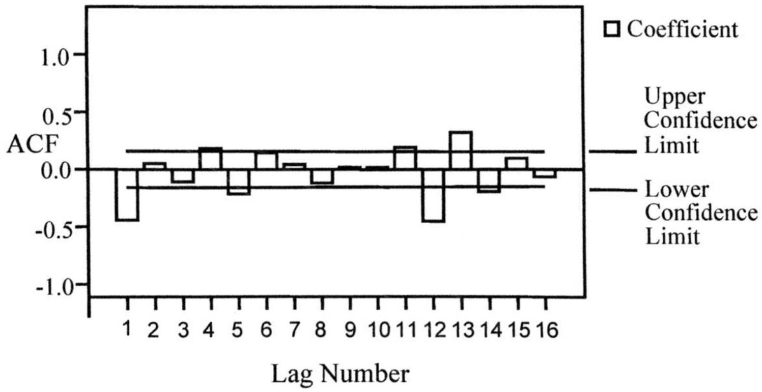

Figure 3.
ACF for PA juvenile DUI arrest rates
ARIMA Model (0, 1, 0)(0, 1, 0)$_{12}$.

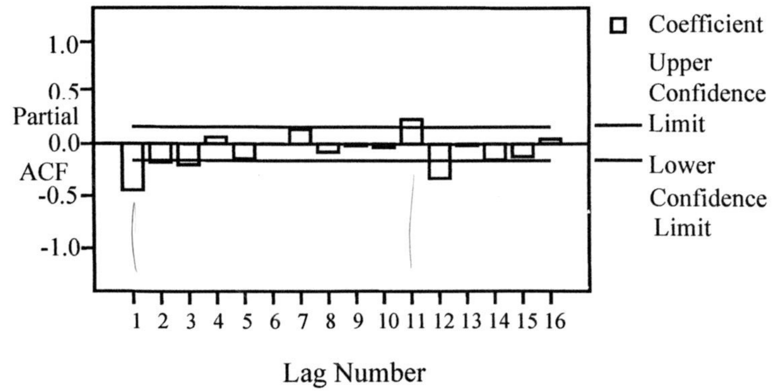

Figure 4.
PACF for PA juvenile DUI arrest rates
ARIMA Model (0, 1, 0) (0, 1, 0)$_{12}$.

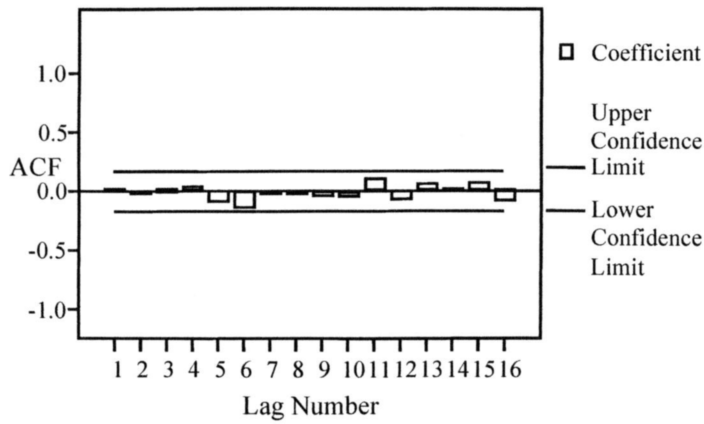

Figure 5.
ACF for PA juvenile DUI arrest rates
ARIMA Model (0, 1, 1)(0, 1, 1)$_{12}$.

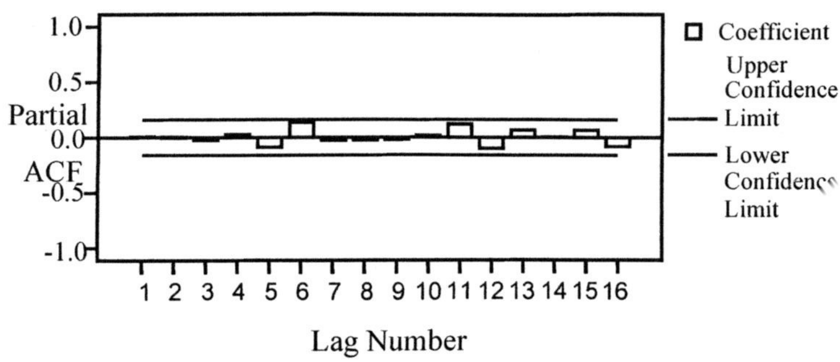

Figure 6.
PACF for PA juvenile DUI arrest rates
ARIMA Model (0, 1, 1)(0, 1, 1)$_{12}$.

Table 2 displays that the value of θ_1 is .557 ($p < .000$), which is within the limits of invertibility ($-1 < \theta_1 < 1$). The value of θ_{12} is .749 ($p < .000$), which also is within the limits of invertibility ($-1 < \theta_{12} < 1$).

For this model, the current observation equals a random shock minus both .557 of the previous month's random shock and .749 of the random shock that occurred last year in the same month ($Y_t = a_t - \theta_1 a_1 - \theta_{12} a_{12}$). The Box-Ljung *Q* statistic for the ACF is not significant at the .05 level. The Box-Ljung *Q* statistic is a measure of residual autocorrelation at each lag within the model. The Box-Ljung *Q* statistic is .938 at Lag 1 and remain insignificant through lag 48 (.230).

Table 2.
SPSS Time Series Regression Output for PA Juvenile DUI Arrest Rates ARIMA Model (0, 1, 1)(0, 1, 1)$_{12}$

MODEL: (0, 1, 1)(0, 1, 1)$_{12}$
Variable: PAJUVDUI
Regressors: PALAWENF
FINAL PARAMETERS:
Number of residuals 155
Standard error 4.6563075
Log likelihood -462.06478
AIC 930.12955
SBC 939.25983

Analysis of Variance:

	DF	Adj. Sum of Squares	Residual Variance
Residuals	152	3521.2341	21.681200

Variables in the Model:

	B	SEB	T-RATIO	PROB.
MA1	.557	.066	.448	.000
SMA1	.749	.076	9.834	.000
PALAWENF	13.957	3.628	3.848	.000

For this model, juvenile drunk driving arrest rates increased an average of 13.96 arrests per month for each 100,000 Pennsylvania licensed juvenile drivers after Pennsylvania started to enforce the juvenile zero-tolerance drunk driving law ($p < .000$). Although this is a significant increase in juvenile drunk driving arrest rates, the true effects are actually masked by the trend's gradual onset to a more permanent stochastic trend established around January 2000 (Figure 7).

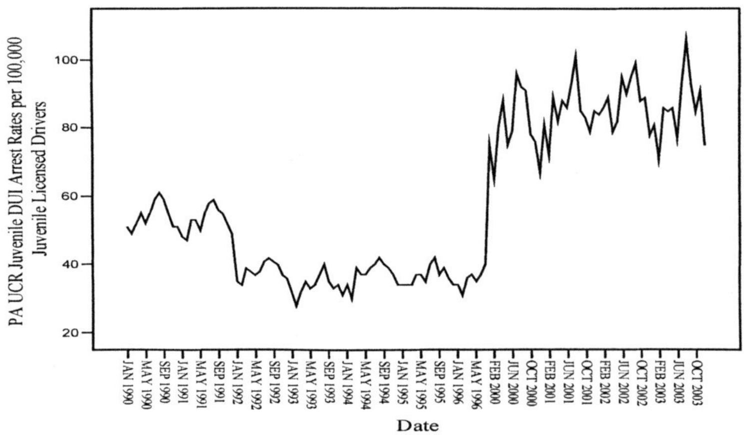

Figure 7.
Sequence plot of Pennsylvania's monthly juvenile drunk driving arrest rates omitting August 1996 through December 1999.

Using a "step function" the value of each post-intervention observation can be identified while controlling for previous post-observations. A more accurate effect of the law's impact can be identified by estimating the difference between the Y-intercept of the pre-intervention observations and the Y-intercept of the post-intervention observations, while controlling for the change in slope from August 1996 through December 1999.

For this model, the change in the Y-intercept between the pre-intervention observations and the stochastic post-intervention observations indicates that juvenile drunk driving arrest rates stabilized after increasing an average of 33.7 arrests per month for each 100,000 Pennsylvania licensed juvenile drivers after Pennsylvania started to enforce the juvenile zero-tolerance drunk driving law ($p < .000$).

Model 2 – Pennsylvania Juvenile Driver Fatality Accident Rates. Figure 8 displays a sequence plot of Pennsylvania juvenile drivers killed in vehicles accidents from January 1990 through December 2003 per 100,000 licensed juvenile drivers. The vertical line indicates the point where Pennsylvania's zero-tolerance juvenile drunk driving law became enforceable (August 1, 1996).

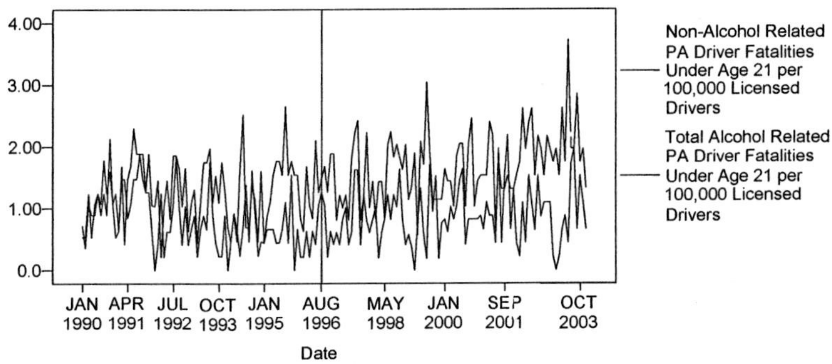

Figure 8.
Sequence plot of Pennsylvania juvenile driver fatalities per 100,000 licensed juvenile drivers.

Figure 8 indicates the presence of a non-stochastic process. A visual inspection of sequence plot shows that from January 1990 through most of 1993, both juvenile driver alcohol and non- alcohol related fatality rates were very similar in quantity and trend. Starting in late 1993 through the remainder of the observations, non-alcohol related juvenile driver fatality rates increased, while alcohol related juvenile driver fatality rates remained stable throughout the observations with the exception of a decline in late 1993 and 1994. At the point where the zero-tolerance juvenile drunk driving law became enforceable, no trend is visually identifiable, in that both sets of observations appear to continue along the trend established in 1993/1994.

Further, Figure 8 displays the presence of seasonality. Annually, for non-alcohol related juvenile driver fatalities, June has the highest fatality rates, followed by July, August, November, and May. Alcohol related juvenile driver fatalities are highest in August, followed closely by July, October, and September, which mirrors the months for highest juvenile drunk driving arrests. Figure 8 indicates a non-stochastic process, so the observations must be differenced, to include a seasonal differencing component.

Table 3 (below) displays the results of Pennsylvania's alcohol related juvenile driver fatality accident rates using an ARIMA model $(0, 1, 1)(0, 1, 1)_{12}$. The value of θ_1 and θ_{12} are within the limits of invertibility.

For this model, the current observation equals a random shock minus both .909 of the previous month's random shock and .979 of the random shock that occurred last year in the same month ($Y_t = a_t - \theta_1 a_1 - \theta_{12} a_{12}$). The Box-Ljung *Q* statistic for the ACF is not significant at the .05 level. The Box-Ljung *Q* statistic is .296 at Lag 1 and remain insignificant through lag 48 (.957).

For this model, juvenile alcohol related driver fatality rates, where the juvenile had consumed any amount of alcohol, increased an average of .2202 fatalities per month for each 100,000 Pennsylvania licensed juvenile drivers after Pennsylvania started to enforce the juvenile zero-tolerance drunk driving law ($p < .266$). Although there is better than a one in four chance that the difference between pre- and post-intervention observations are unrelated to the enactment of the law; if it were to hold true, a trend increase of approximately one fatality per month occurred after the law was enacted, than would have been predicted based on pre-intervention trends. Additional statistical analysis indicates that enactment of the zero-tolerance juvenile drunk driving law had no significant impact on the fatality rate trends for Pennsylvania juvenile drivers who had a BAC of 0, .01 - .09, or .10 or higher.

Table 3.
SPSS Time Series Regression Output for PA Intoxicated Juvenile Driver Fatality Rates
ARIMA Model (0, 1, 1)(0, 1, 1)$_{12}$

	B	SEB	T-RATIO	PROB.
MA1	.909	.038	24.124	.000
SMA1	.979	.476	2.060	.041
PALAWENF	.220	.197	1.116	.266

Model 3 – Pennsylvania Adult Drunk Driving Arrest Rates. Model 1 indicated a significant increase in juvenile drunk driving arrest rates after the implementation of Pennsylvania's zero-tolerance juvenile drunk driving law. The intent of the remaining three ITS designs is to rule out the plausibility that the observed increase in juvenile drunk driving arrest rates was caused by factors other than the law's implementation. Model 3 assesses the impact this law had on Pennsylvania adult drunk driving arrest rates. The hypothesis is that since the law was not intended to affect adult drivers, there should be no interruption in the established adult drunk driving arrest rate pattern surrounding the period the law became enforceable. If there is an increase in adult drunk driving arrest rates during this period, it is plausible that enforcement issues/levels were at least part of the explanation for increases in both juvenile and adult drunk driving arrests.

The vertical line in Figure 9 represents the zero-tolerance juvenile drunk driving law implementation date. A visual observation of Figure 9 suggests that Pennsylvania's adult drunk driving arrest rates were not affected by this law.

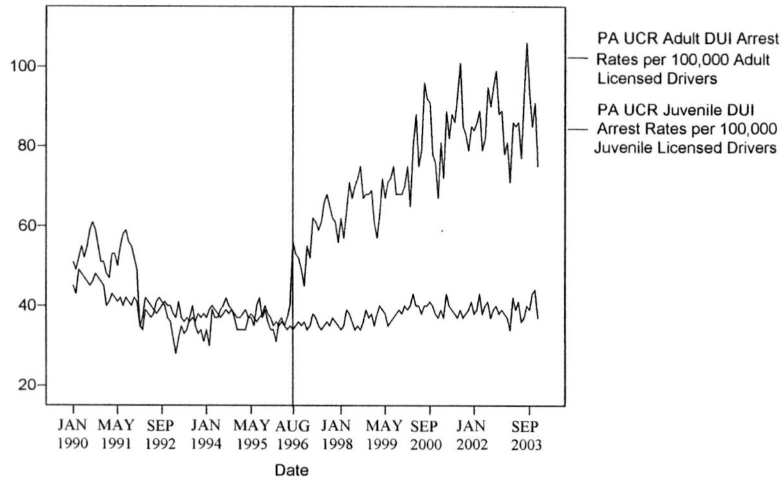

Figure 9.
Sequence plot of Pennsylvania juvenile and adult drunk driving arrest rates per 100,000 licensed drivers.

Using an ARIMA model $(0, 1, 1)(0, 1, 1)_{12}$, a regression equation adds validity to the visual observation that the enforcement of Pennsylvania's zero-tolerance juvenile drunk driving law had no impact on Pennsylvania's adult drunk driving arrest rates. For this model, adult drunk driving arrests rates decreased at a rate of about .76 per 100,000 licensed PA adult drivers between pre- and post-intervention arrest rates, where the intervention point was defined as the enforcement date of Pennsylvania's zero-tolerance juvenile drunk driving law. Table 4 displays that the change in pre- and post- intervention arrest rates for adult drunk drivers is insignificant ($p > .516$). The value of θ_1 and θ_{12} are within the limits of invertibility.

The value for the constant is .026 ($p > .132$), which is not statistically significant so this parameter was dropped from the model. The Box-Ljung *Q* statistic for this model is .783 at Lag 1 and remain insignificant through lag 48 (.771).

Table 4.
SPSS Time Series Regression Output for PA Adult DUI Arrest Rates ARIMA Model $(0, 1, 1)(0, 1, 1)_{12}$

	B	SEB	T-RATIO	PROB.
MA1	.601	.064	9.430	.000
SMA1	.684	.081	8.489	.000
PALAWENF	-.758	1.164	-.651	.516

Model 4 – Pennsylvania Juvenile Arrests for Alcohol Offenses other than Drunk Driving. Model 4 assesses the impact, if any, the Pennsylvania zero-tolerance juvenile drunk driving law had on Pennsylvania juveniles who were charged with other alcohol related incidents other than drunk driving. The hypothesis is that since the law was intended to deter juveniles from consuming alcohol and driving, it should have no effect on other juvenile alcohol related offenses. If there was an increase in other juvenile alcohol related arrests during this period, it is plausible that enforcement issues/levels were at least part of the explanation for increases in both juvenile drunk driving arrests and juvenile arrests for other alcohol related incidents.

The vertical line in Figure 10 (below) represents the zero-tolerance juvenile drunk driving law implementation date. A visual observation of Figure 10 indicates that Pennsylvania juvenile arrest rates for other alcohol related incidents did not appear to be affected by this law.

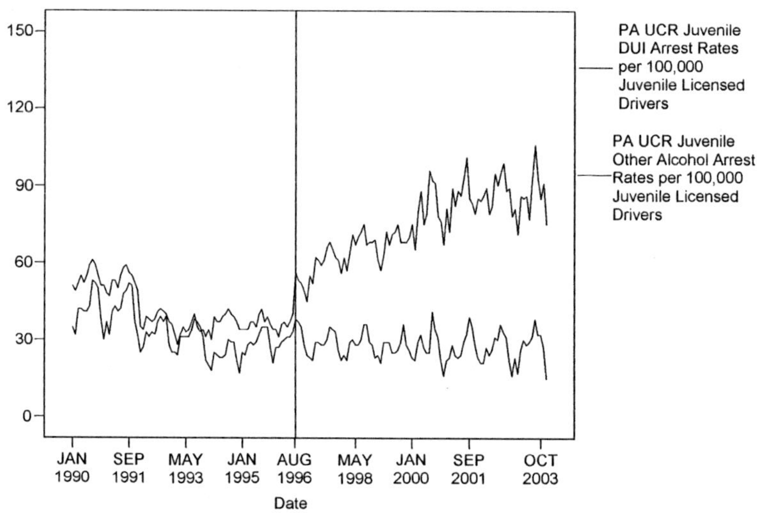

Figure 10.
Sequence plot of Pennsylvania juvenile drunk driving arrest rates and juvenile arrest rates for other alcohol related incidents per 100,000 licensed juvenile drivers.

Using an ARIMA model $(0, 1, 1)(0, 1, 1)_{12}$, a regression equation adds validity to the visual observation that the enforcement of Pennsylvania's zero-tolerance juvenile drunk driving law had no impact on Pennsylvania's juvenile arrest rates for other alcohol related incidents.

Table 5 (below) indicates that for this model, the juvenile arrest rate for "other alcohol related offenses" decreased at a rate of about .628 per 100,000 licensed PA juvenile drivers between pre- and post-intervention arrest rates, where the intervention point was defined as the enforcement date of Pennsylvania's zero-tolerance juvenile drunk driving law. Table 5 displays that the change in pre- and post- intervention juvenile arrest rates for other alcohol related offenses is insignificant ($p > .811$). The value for the constant is .012 ($p > .712$), which is not statistically significant, so this parameter was dropped from the model. The value of θ_1 and θ_{12} are within the limits of invertibility. The Box-Ljung *Q* statistic for this model is .218 at Lag 1 and remain insignificant through lag 48 (.863

Table 5.
SPSS Time Series Regression Output for PA Juvenile Arrest Rates for Alcohol Related Offenses other than DUI ARIMA Model $(0, 1, 1)(0, 1, 1)_{12}$

	B	SEB	T-RATIO	PROB.
MA1	.401	.070	5.693	.000
SMA1	.964	.299	3.226	.002
PALAWENF	-.628	2.624	-.239	.811

Model 5 – Switching Replication Model using Ohio and Pennsylvania's Juvenile OVI/DUI Arrest Rates.

Table 2 (page 109) indicated that Pennsylvania's lowering of the drunk driving BAC level for juveniles to .02 mg/ml significantly increased the juvenile drunk driving arrest rates in that state. Model 5 assesses the impact Pennsylvania's zero-tolerance juvenile DUI law (August 1996) had on Ohio juvenile driver OVI (operating a vehicle under the influence) arrest rates. The model also assesses the impact that Ohio's zero-tolerance juvenile OVI law (May 1994) had on Ohio and Pennsylvania juvenile driver OVI/DUI arrest rates. The hypothesis was that the implementation of each state's law would not impact the juvenile OVI/DUI arrest rates in the adjoining state. If there was a significant increase or decrease in OVI/DUI arrest rates in either state at the time the other enacted its law, it is plausible that some historical event has occurred in both law enforcement jurisdictions which would be at least part of the explanation for increases or decreases affecting the neighboring state's juvenile OVI/DUI arrest rates.

The vertical lines in Figure 11 indicate the implementation dates for Ohio and Pennsylvania's zero-tolerance juvenile OVI/DUI laws. A visual observation of Figure 11 indicates that the two laws did affect the juvenile OVI/DUI arrest rates within their jurisdiction, but do not appear to have affected the other state's juvenile OVI/DUI arrest rates. Using ARIMA modeling, a regression equation adds validity to the visual observation that the enactment of the law by each state did not impact the neighboring state's juvenile OVI/DUI arrest rates.

Although Ohio data was not available before June 1993, a visual inspection of the obtainable data suggests that while Ohio's juvenile OVI law had no impact on Pennsylvania juvenile DUI arrest rates, it did have an immediate and abrupt, but temporary effect on Ohio juvenile OVI arrest rates. The data indicates that Ohio juvenile OVI monthly arrest rates per 100,000 licensed juvenile drivers almost doubled from May 1994 through December 1994, before returning to a slightly higher level than their pre-intervention levels, which was maintained through December 2003.

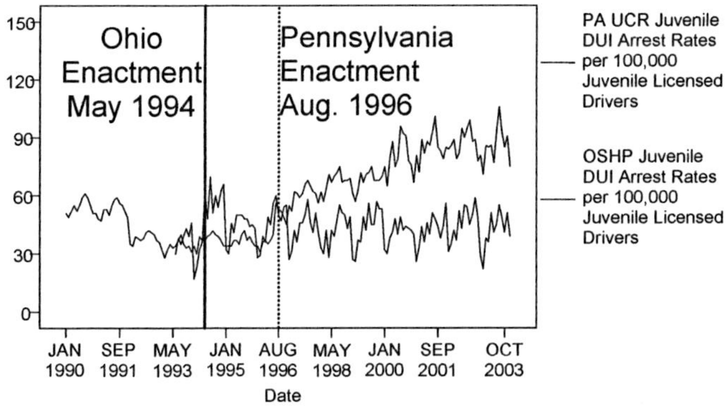

Figure 11.
Sequence plot of Pennsylvania and Ohio's monthly juvenile drunk driving/operating a vehicle while intoxicated arrest rates.

A descriptive and statistical analysis indicates that for the 11 month period prior to the enactment of the Ohio law (June 1993 – April 1994) juvenile monthly DUI/OVI arrest rates per 100,000 licensed juvenile drivers averaged 34.91 (Md. 34, SD. 3.113) in Pennsylvania and 34.36 (Md. 36, SD. 8.5) in Ohio. For the 8 month period immediately following the Ohio law implementation (May – December 1994) juvenile monthly DUI/OVI arrest rates per 100,000 licensed juvenile drivers averaged 38.5 (Md. 39, SD. 2.449) in Pennsylvania and 59.13 (Md. 61, SD. 7.549) in Ohio. After December 1994, the Ohio OVI arrest rates maintained a similar trend through December 2003, with an average monthly arrest rate of 43.23 per 100,000 licensed juvenile drivers (Md. 44.0, SD. 8.551).

Table 6 (below) indicates that prior to the enforcement of Ohio's zero-tolerance OVI law, after modeling for auto correlation [ARIMA model (2, 0, 0)(2, 0, $0)_{12}$], the average monthly arrest rate per 100,000 licensed juvenile drivers was 32.59 (constant). The impact of the law appeared to be significant ($p < .000$) in that the monthly juvenile OVI arrest rates increased by 12.57 per 100,000 licensed juvenile drivers. The value for each variable in the model was significant and remained within the limits of stationarity. The AR_2 component was omitted since it was identified as insignificant in this model (.154, $p > .082$). The Box-Ljung *Q* statistic for this model is .700 at Lag 1 and remain insignificant through lag 48 (.126).

Table 6.
SPSS Time Series Regression Output for OH Juvenile OVI Arrest Rates using OH Zero-Tolerance Enforcement Date as the Interruption Point ARIMA Model (2, 0, 0)(2, 0, $0)_{12}$

	B	SEB	T-RATIO	PROB.
AR1	.343	.082	4.170	.000
SAR1	.430	.079	5.416	.000
SAR2	.387	.084	4.608	.000
OHLAWENF	12.571	2.643	4.757	.000
CONSTANT	32.587	3.587	9.086	.000

In maintaining a similar trend after January 1995, the Ohio juvenile OVI arrest rates do not appear to have been impacted by the enactment of Pennsylvania's zero-tolerance juvenile drunk driving law. Table 7 displays that Ohio's monthly juvenile OVI arrest rates increased from 41.43 to 41.98 per 100,000 licensed juvenile drivers, where the intervention point was defined as the enforcement date of Pennsylvania's zero-tolerance juvenile drunk driving law. Table 7 displays that the change in pre- and post-intervention monthly juvenile OVI arrest rates for licensed juvenile Ohio drivers is insignificant ($p > .872$). The value for each variable in the model was significant and remained within the limits of stationarity. The Box-Ljung *Q* statistic for this model is .637 at Lag 1 and remain insignificant through lag 48 (.534).

Table 7.
SPSS Time Series Regression Output for OH Juvenile OVI Arrest Rates using PA Zero-Tolerance Enforcement Date as the Interruption Point ARIMA Model (2, 0, 0)(2, 0, 0)$_{12}$

	B	SEB	T-RATIO	PROB.
AR1	.385	.086	4.489	.000
AR2	.209	.089	2.345	.020
SAR1	.410	.078	5.226	.000
SAR2	.408	.085	4.808	.000
PALAWENF	.549	3.404	.161	.872
CONSTANT	41.431	5.376	7.706	.000

Similar to Ohio's unchanging juvenile OVI arrest rates at the time Pennsylvania enacted its zero-tolerance juvenile DUI laws, Pennsylvania's juvenile DUI arrest rates appear to have been unaffected by the Ohio juvenile OVI law. A visual inspection of Figure 11 (above), supported by statistical analysis (Table 8) suggests that from January 1992 through July 1996, Pennsylvania's juvenile DUI arrest rates remained relatively constant and were not affected by the enactment of Ohio's zero-tolerance juvenile OVI law.

Table 8.
SPSS Time Series Regression Output for PA Juvenile DUI Arrest Rates using OH Zero-Tolerance Enforcement Date as the Interruption Point ARIMA Model (0, 1, 1)(2, 1, 1)$_{12}$

	B	SEB	T-RATIO	PROB.
MA1	.492	.069	7.121	.000
SMA	1.782	.077	10.158	.000
OHLAWENF	.435	4.012	.108	.914

Table 8 indicates that Pennsylvania's monthly juvenile DUI arrest rates were unaffected by the implementation of Ohio's juvenile OVI law. The change in pre- and post-intervention monthly juvenile DUI arrest rates for Pennsylvania licensed juvenile drivers is insignificant ($p > .913$). Table 8 displays that the value of θ_1 and θ_{12} are within the limits of invertibility. The value for the constant is .057 ($p > .345$), which is not statistically significant, so this parameter was dropped from the model. The Box-Ljung *Q* statistic for this model is .964 at Lag 1 and remain insignificant through lag 48 (.164).

Model 6 – Switching Replication Model using Ohio and Pennsylvania's Juvenile Driver Fatality Accident Rates. Model 6 is identical to Model 5 except the variable of interest is changed from OVI/DUI arrest rates to alcohol-related juvenile driver fatality accident rates (Figure 12). The outcome from the data is listed in Tables 9, 10, and 11.

Table 9 (below) indicates that Pennsylvania's monthly alcohol related juvenile driver fatality rates were unaffected by the implementation of Ohio's juvenile OVI law. The change in pre- and post- intervention monthly alcohol related juvenile driver fatality rates for Pennsylvania licensed juvenile drivers is insignificant ($p > .635$). The value of θ_1 is within the limits of invertibility. The value for the constant is .001 (p > .191) and the value of θ_{12} is .983 (p > .101), both of which are not statistically significant so these parameters were dropped from the model. The Box-Ljung *Q* statistic is .361 at Lag 1 and remain insignificant through lag 48 (.957).

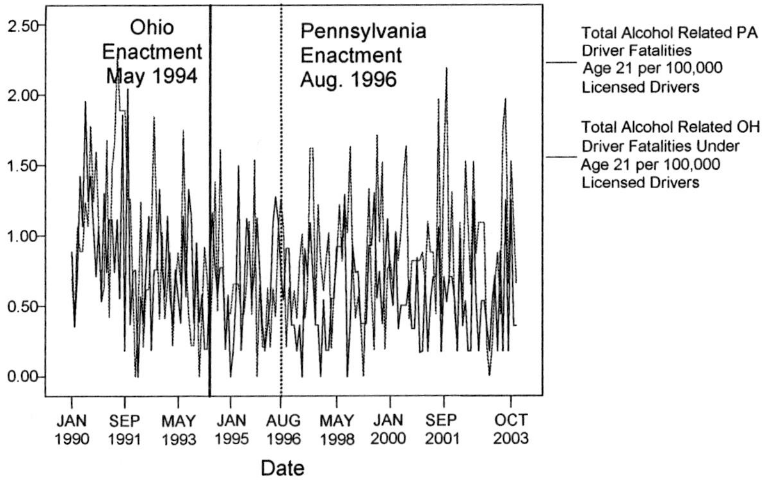

Figure 12.
Sequence plot of Pennsylvania and Ohio's alcohol related juvenile driver fatalities per 100,000 licensed juvenile drivers.

Table 9.
SPSS Time Series Regression Output for PA Intoxicated Juvenile Driver Fatality Rates using OH Zero-Tolerance OVI Enforcement Date as the Interruption Point
ARIMA Model (0, 1, 1)(0, 1, 1)$_{12}$

	B	SEB	T-RATIO	PROB.
MA	1.900	.039	23.090	.000
OHLAWENF	-.098	.206	-.475	.636

Table 10 indicates that Ohio's zero-tolerance juvenile drunk driving legislation did not significantly impact Ohio's monthly alcohol related juvenile driver fatality rates. The change in pre- and post- intervention monthly alcohol related juvenile driver fatality rates for Ohio licensed juvenile drivers is insignificant ($p > .397$). The value of ϕ_1 is within the limits of stationarity, and θ_1 and θ_{12} are within the limits of invertibility. The Box-Ljung *Q* statistic is .799 at Lag 1 and remain insignificant through lag 48 (.289).

Table 10.
SPSS Time Series Regression Output for OH Intoxicated Juvenile Driver Fatality Rates using OH Zero-Tolerance OVI Enforcement Date as the Interruption Point
ARIMA Model (1, 1, 1)(0, 1, 1)$_{12}$

	B	SEB	T-RATIO	PROB.
AR1	-.159	.076	-2.094	.038
MA1	.968	.038	25.666	.000
SMA1	.944	.163	5.812	.000
OHLAWENF	.100	.118	.848	.398
CONSTANT	.000	.000	2.083	.039

Table 11 indicates that Ohio's monthly alcohol related juvenile driver fatality rates were unaffected by the implementation of Pennsylvania's juvenile DUI law. The change in pre- and post- intervention monthly alcohol related juvenile driver fatality rates for Ohio licensed juvenile drivers is insignificant ($p > .451$). The value of ϕ_1 is within the limits of stationarity, and θ_1 and θ_{12} are within the limits of invertibility. The Box-Ljung *Q* statistic is .834 at Lag 1 and remain insignificant through lag 48 (.417).

Table 11.
SPSS Time Series Regression Output for OH Intoxicated Juvenile Driver Fatality Rates using PA Zero-Tolerance DUI Enforcement Date as the Interruption Point
ARIMA Model (1, 1, 1)(0, 1, 1)$_{12}$

	B	SEB	T-RATIO	PROB.
AR1	-.183	.080	-2.277	.024
MA1	.910	.043	20.960	.000
SMA1	.911	.108	8.431	.000
PALAWENF	-.103	.137	-.755	.451

Statistical Summary

Statistical analyses of the data suggest that the implementation of zero-tolerance juvenile drunk driving laws had the impact of significantly increasing the arrest rates for this offense. The data holds true for both Pennsylvania and Ohio, with the difference being that Ohio juvenile OVI arrest rates dropped slightly after peaking, where Pennsylvania's juvenile DUI arrest rates maintained the significantly higher arrest rate level. Fatality accident rates involving juvenile drunk drivers were not significantly impacted in either state by the enactment of juvenile OVI/DUI legislation. The variables used to control for threats to validity (e.g., PA adult DUI arrest rates, other PA juvenile alcohol related offenses) also were not significantly impacted by the implementation of Pennsylvania's zero-tolerance juvenile drunk driving law.

Qualitative Analysis

Policy implementation and enforcement. Although not the primary means of evaluation for this legal impact study, the data obtained from the informal, semi-structured interviews with law enforcement supervisors helped control for various threats to validity. The most plausible validity threats related to implementation and enforcement were identified as: 1) unreliability of treatment implementation; 2) selection bias, specifically the targeting of juvenile offenders, and 3) treatment diffusion. Questions one and six were designed to solicit information about the perceived effectiveness of the law from the law enforcement supervisors' perspectives. There were two common themes identified from the responses to these questions.

The first theme was that the law was enforced as written, and it was not appropriate to enforce or fail to enforce laws that individual officers strongly supported or opposed. The response was as expected since it would be politically incorrect to acknowledge selective enforcement of various laws. Additionally, the data suggest that since the arrest rates for juvenile drinking and driving did increase substantially in Pennsylvania after the law was passed that law enforcement officers were enforcing the law.

The second theme addressing the perception of the law's effectiveness from the law enforcement supervisors' perspectives was that the law is a starting point to make the public more aware of the dangers of drinking and driving, but to be effective the law needed to garner public support. The law enforcement supervisors acknowledged that without public support for the zero-tolerance juvenile drunk driving law, legal sanctions would have a minimal impact in deterring this offense.

The supervisors' assessments supported those of Skinner (1953) and Tittle and Logan (1973) where it was suggested that laws that are not supported by strong societal norms often are disobeyed regardless of the legal sanctions. The data suggest that even though juvenile drinking and driving arrest rates increased substantially immediately after the law was enacted, the arrest rates failed to decline after the certainty of getting stopped and arrested increased. The data indicate that the arrest rates peaked about three years after the law was initiated and have remained constant at that level.

Question 2 – 5 addressed the plausible validity threats related to implementation, selection bias, and treatment diffusion, which could be associated with the zero-tolerance juvenile drunk driving law. The underlying themes identified from the responses to these questions were that: 1) although juvenile drunk drivers were not a specific target for enforcement, a clear message was being sent to juveniles about the seriousness of drinking any amount of alcohol and then making the decision to operate a motor vehicle; 2) no internal or external pressure was applied to law enforcement supervisors to either aggressively enforce or refrain from enforcing this law or other laws related to juvenile alcohol use; and 3) there were no implementation or enforcement issues with this law.

The law enforcement interviews supported the patterns observed in the quantitative data. Law enforcement supervisors indicated that they perceived no issues that should have affected treatment implementation. The immediate, gradual increase in the juvenile drunk driving arrest data supports this theme. Law enforcement supervisors also indicated that they perceived no issues that would have caused juveniles to be differentially targeted as a result of this law, which addresses both selection bias and treatment diffusion. The data on adult drunk driving arrest rates and juvenile arrest rates for other alcohol related offenses other than drunk driving support the interview data. The failure of adult drunk driving arrest rates and juvenile arrest rates for other alcohol related offenses other than drunk driving to react to the implementation of the zero-tolerance juvenile drunk driving law suggests that juveniles were not targeted, at least for other alcohol related offenses, and that general enforcement of drunk driving laws remained unchanged between pre- and post-treatment observations.

The thematic content of the interview data indicate that there were no perceived issues related to this law's implementation or enforcement. The quantitative data also indicate that there were no unexplainable anomalies in the trend of the data, which would suggest implementation or enforcement issues. The implementation trends of the zero-tolerance juvenile drunk driving laws in both Ohio and Pennsylvania appear very similar. In both states the juvenile arrest rates immediately and gradually increased after the law was enforceable. The congruency between the qualitative and quantitative data enhances the statistical conclusion and internal validity of this research.

Media effect. The presence of a media effect in the data would be most plausible in the pre-treatment observations immediately preceding the intervention (Ross, 1982). The effect would be indicated by a drop in juvenile drunk driving arrest rates or juvenile fatality accident rates just prior to the law's enforcement date. Hypothetically, pre-treatment media coverage about the law would increase individual awareness and would restrict offending. A media effect, if present, could affect the location of the y-intercept at the time the law was enforceable and could impact the trend in both the pre- and post-treatment observations immediately surrounding the treatment area.

A search was conducted in 32 newspapers published in Pennsylvania (Appendix B) and press releases from the Pennsylvania Liquor Control Board (PLCB). The search focused on any newspaper article or PLCB press release printed between August 1995 and September 2005 that related to "zero-tolerance" "underage drinking" or "fatality accidents." The search resulted in 14 newspaper articles (See Table 12 below) and 90 PLCB press releases being identified as related to the search criteria. Although 13 of the PLCB press releases specifically addressed zero-tolerance for underage drinking and an additional 12 addressed increased enforcement of drunk driving laws, no press releases were identified that specifically addressed the zero-tolerance juvenile drunk driving law.

The data (Figure 9) indicate that the media had little, if any effect, on the pre- and post-treatment observations surrounding the time period the zero-tolerance law was implemented. The archival search adds validity to the quantitative data in that only 3 newspapers, of the 32 searched, printed pre-enforcement articles informing the public about the new law. Additionally, 2 newspapers accounted for 10 of the 14 pre- or post-enforcement articles located that informed the public about Pennsylvania's zero-tolerance juvenile alcohol law. The perceived lack of media coverage, along with the trend in the quantitative data resulted in the threat of a media impact on the data being cautiously discarded.

A common theme that appeared in the post-enactment newspaper articles was that the articles were primarily related to a political candidate who was appearing publicly with a representative from MADD. This trend was most prevalent in the *Lancaster New Era* where one of the candidates was being heavily supported by MADD (See Table 12). The general theme of the post-enactment articles was that a political opponent had voted against or held opinions against more stringent regulations governing alcohol use in general and specifically alcohol use by juveniles.

Overall, the qualitative archival data supports the quantitative data. The media provided little coverage about the zero-tolerance juvenile alcohol law other than that related the governor signing the legislation and that which was offered as political rhetoric suggesting one candidate was more supportive of the effort than another.

Table 12.
PA Newspaper Articles related to PA Zero-Tolerance Juvenile Drunk Driving Law

DATE	NEWSPAPER	THEME
Nov. 29, 1995	Pittsburgh Post-Gazette	Pre-treatment Public Awareness
June 21, 1996	Lancaster New Era	Pre-treatment Public Awareness
June 25&26, 1996	Erie Times-News	Pre-treatment Public Awareness
July 03&10, Aug 07, 1996	Lancaster New Era	Pre-treatment Public Awareness
Aug. 11, 1996	The Times Leader	Post-treatment Public Awareness
Aug. 26, 1996	Lancaster New Era	Post-treatment Public Awareness
Sept. 19, Nov. 29, 1996	Pittsburgh Post-Gazette	Post-treatment Public Awareness
Feb. 02, 1997	Centre Daily Times	Post-treatment Public Awareness
Dec.02, 1997	Lancaster New Era	Post-treatment Public Awareness
Sep. 22,1998	Lancaster New Era	Post-treatment Public Awareness

Chapter 5

A Problem that cannot be Legislated Away

Analysis Summary

This research is some of the first, if not the first, to empirically assess the impact of the federally mandated zero-tolerance juvenile drunk driving legislation, which was implemented throughout the U.S. The data indicate that, while the certainty and severity of punishment for juvenile drunk driving arrests significantly increased, the legislation was ineffective for reducing juvenile alcohol-related fatality traffic accident rates. These results were observed for both Pennsylvania and Ohio. Further, the ineffectiveness of this federal mandate (lower juvenile BAC limits) to reduce juvenile alcohol related fatality accident rates is similar to the results found in the majority of the research that evaluated the impact of the 1984 federal mandate to increase the minimum drinking age to 21 in an attempt to reduce juvenile alcohol related fatality accident rates (see for e.g., Hilton, 1984; Hingson et al., 1987; Muller, 1989; Ross, McCleary, & Epperlein, 1981).

The effect of the zero-tolerance juvenile drunk driving legislation in Pennsylvania was an 80% increase in juvenile drunk driving arrests. Juvenile drunk driving arrest rates per 100,000 licensed juvenile drivers increased from a monthly pre-intervention average of 41.6 to a post-intervention average of 75. Prior to the legislation, approximately 201 juveniles were being arrested monthly in Pennsylvania for drunk driving; after the legislation, the monthly average increased to 359.

Further, these statistics actually dampen the true impact the legislation had on juvenile drunk driving arrest rates. Immediately following the enactment of the law, juvenile drunk driving arrest rates gradually climbed for several years until a new permanent level, or new y intercept, was established. The inclusion of this 42 month gradual incline reduces the mean value of the established post-intervention y intercept.

Referencing Figure 1 for a graphic explanation, juvenile drunk driving arrest rates had been declining through the early 1990s, until they leveled off around January 1993. As a result of the zero-tolerance juvenile drunk driving law (August 1996), post-intervention juvenile drunk driving arrest rates were increasing until they leveled off around January 2000. Using these two dates as a reference, juvenile drunk driving arrest rates per 100,000 licensed juvenile drivers increased from a monthly pre-intervention average of 35.8 (January 1993 – July 1996) to a monthly post-intervention average of 84.8 (January 2000 – December 2003), a 137% increase.

Despite the strong significant increase in juvenile drunk driving arrest rates, there was no significant impact on monthly juvenile driver fatality rates. Using the enforcement date of the law as the intervention point, monthly non-alcohol related driver fatality traffic accident rates per 100,000 juvenile drivers declined by .019 (p =

.905), where alcohol related juvenile driver fatality traffic accident rates increased by .22 (p = .266). Disaggregating the post-treatment alcohol related juvenile driver fatality traffic accident data revealed that those juvenile drivers who had a BAC between .01 and .09 had an increase in fatality accident rates of .05 per 100,000 licensed juvenile drivers (p = .556). Juvenile drivers who had a BAC .10 or higher also had an increase in fatality accident rates of .17 per 100,000 licensed juvenile drivers (p = .355). As indicated, these increases and decreases were not statistically significant.

The data imply that the increase in juvenile drunk driving arrest rates was not the result of a change in general enforcement efforts, which was supported by the law enforcement interviews. If drunk driving enforcement efforts would have changed, the adult drunk driving arrest rates also would have reacted to such a change, which they did not (-.757, p = .516). Although statistically insignificant, adult drunk driving arrest rates actually declined after the law was enacted. The data further indicate that the increase in juvenile drunk driving arrest rates was not the result of a more encompassing targeting of juvenile alcohol use, which law enforcement interviews also supported. If juvenile alcohol use was targeted, arrest rates for juvenile alcohol related offenses other the drunk driving should have reacted to the change in enforcement, which they did not (-.628, p = .811). Similar to adult drunk driving arrest rates, other juvenile alcohol related arrest rates insignificantly declined after the law was enacted.

The qualitative and quantitative data collected for this research suggests that there was no change in law enforcement efforts or any apparent media effect that would obscure the impact of Pennsylvania's juvenile zero-tolerance drunk driving law. The impact of this law was to significantly increase juvenile drunk driving arrest rates, while having little or no apparent impact on juvenile fatality vehicle accident rates. A similar pattern was displayed for Ohio's juvenile zero-tolerance drunk driving law, in that juvenile arrest rates increased with no impact on juvenile fatality vehicle accident rates.

Ineffective Legislation

This research supports the observations made by Paternoster (1987) that "perceptions of the certainty and severity of punishment do not seem to deter trivial and infrequent behaviors of high school and university students" (p. 214). Further, it supports a conclusion that our current deterrence approach to preventing underage drinking, which relies heavily on the fear of legal sanctions, appears ineffective. Both the uniformed drinking age laws and now, the zero-tolerance juvenile drunk driving laws, at least in Pennsylvania, have failed to deter a significant amount of juveniles from consuming alcohol (Johnston, 2004; PCCD, 2004) and have failed to significantly reduce alcohol related juvenile fatality traffic accidents (Fatality Analysis Reporting System, 2003). A key question not addressed by Paternoster (1987), which will be explored here, is why deterrence based policies and laws seem to fail to deter infrequent behaviors such as juvenile DUI.

Multiple studies have indicated that our deterrence-based policy approach to preventing juvenile alcohol use is not working (e.g., Hilton, 1984; Levy, 2002; Pogarsky, 2002; Shope & Bingham, 2002). This study supplies additional support that a zero-tolerance approach, while significantly increasing juvenile drunk driving arrest rates, appears ineffective in lowering juvenile alcohol-related traffic fatalities. Further, the data in this study support Skinner's (1953) assertion that individual behavior is not learned or changed simply by a governmental agency codifying its controlling practices. Although the legal sanctions for juvenile drinking and driving were increased, this did not translate into a reduction in offending. Based on a review of the literature, three plausible explanations (social consensus, developmental, and causation) will be discussed as to why empirical support for deterrence theory as it relates to underage drinking and juvenile drunk driving appears ineffective.

Social Consensus. The first explanation relates to whether these laws developed from consensus or by social reaction. In attempting to deter infrequent behaviors, Reynolds, Seydlitz, and Jenkins (2000) found that for a juvenile curfew law to work in preventing crime, juveniles must be a large percentage of the offenders. If laws are designed to target infrequent behavior, their impact will be minimal at best. The Pennsylvania zero tolerance juvenile drunk driving law targeted juvenile offenders who had a BAC level between .01 and .09. In 1996, when the law was enacted, these juveniles accounted for 0.6% of all the drivers killed in vehicle accidents and 1.4% of all drivers killed in alcohol-related vehicle accidents. Further, this group accounted for only 1.4% of the all the individuals killed in motor vehicle accidents (driver, passenger, pedestrian, or bicyclist). Finally, between 1990 and 2003, an annual average of only 2.6% of all alcohol related fatality accidents involved a juvenile driver with a BAC between .01 and .09 (Lorenzo Daniels - FARS Statistician, personal communication, August 31, 2005).

For Pennsylvania, the zero tolerance juvenile drunk driving law failed to target 97% of the drivers involved in alcohol related vehicle fatalities. Such statistics might lead one to ask why a law was enacted to target such a small category of offenders. This question, along with "why is Pennsylvania's zero-tolerance juvenile drunk driving law ineffective in controlling juvenile drunk driving and the corresponding fatality accidents?", may have the same theoretical response.

In addressing the first question as to why such a small category of offenders were targeted, legislatures, especially at the federal level, are heavily lobbied by multiple special interest groups. By voicing their interests at the national level, these groups can rapidly and cost-effectively affect legislation in all 50 states. In support of this claim, at least for this particular issue, both the uniformed drinking age and the juvenile zero-tolerance drunk driving legislation were federal mandates to the states, with the threat of lost federal highway funds for the lack of compliance. The "facts" these special interest groups use to sell their agenda to legislatures may be well intentioned but also ideologically motivated and/or biased (Weitzer, 2005).

In the case of juvenile drunk driving, the official statistics suggest that the problem may not be as severe as stated and empirical research coming from academia indicates that the legislative remedies are having little or no impact in reducing the rate of offending. Further, it is plausible that the legislative remedies, fought for by special interest groups, could be actually compounding the problem. By highly publicizing the juvenile drunk driving fatality rate and targeting juvenile drivers, without placing it in perspective (less than 3 % of all fatality accidents involve a juvenile with a BAC between .01 and .09), the issue is perceived as a more severe problem than it really is. Since it is deemed a real problem, legislation is passed, which increases punishment and the crime rate, but fails to resolve the problem. The reason the problem is not resolved is that it is not real, but only perceived. Beccaria (1764/1986) noted that deterrence-based policies will be ineffective in these situations. "To prohibit a host of harmless acts is not to prevent the crimes to which they might lead; it is, rather, to create new crimes; it is to define virtue and vice (which are preached to us as eternal and immutable) at one's whim" (p. 74).

Mothers Against Drunk Driving (MADD) offers an example of the power certain lobbying groups can have with federal, state, and local legislatures and agencies. MADD's Annual Report (Hamilton, 2004), highlights the influence this organization has had regarding legislation involving alcohol. The report notes that: 1) awards were given to journalists and media outlets (e.g., Dateline and Good Morning America) who advanced MADD's mission; 2) U.S. Department of Justice funding was granted to promote MADD's mission; 3) during 2004, MADD representatives appeared before Congress addressing three separate issues (underage drinking legislation (twice) and increased resources for drunk driving law enforcement; 4) MADD sponsored the Law Enforcement Leader Summit, which addressed increased law enforcement visibility to deter drunk drivers; 5) MADD engaged in two separate activities with the NHTSA; 6) MADD developed and implemented a 35-minute multi media campaign in schools about underage drinking prevention; 7) MADD obtained OJJDP funds to sponsor nationwide 20 additional youth groups in an attempt to deter underage drinking; 8) MADD expanded the University MADD program to campuses in Florida, Tennessee, Maryland, Kentucky, and Texas; 9) MADD announced the winners of the annual MADD

National President's Award (e.g., Outstanding Law Enforcement Award, Ralph W. Hingson Research in Practice Award, Jean Moorhead Duffy Award for Legislative Initiative, Criminal Justice Award); 10) MADD received 10.576 million dollars in government grants and received a total revenue of 53.784 million dollars for the fiscal year of 2003-2004. Additionally, MADD periodically releases drunk driving report cards for each state, rating their efficiency in passing drunk driving legislation and deterring underage drinking and drunk driving. These reports cards are made public knowledge through the MADD home page and are released to the media.

In the archival data reviewed for this research, MADD was mentioned in 7 of the 14 news articles. In 5 of the articles, MADD was offering support for the zero-tolerance juvenile drunk driving legislation, and in 2, they were soliciting support to lower the adult BAC level from the recently established .08 mg/ml to .05 mg/ml. Pennsylvania Liquor Control Board (PLCB) press releases between November 1996 and August 2001 also mentioned MADD on multiple occasions. MADD was commended by the PLCB and then First Lady Michele Ridge for its selection of 21 Pennsylvania students to attend its national youth summit related to preventing underage drinking. Multiple press releases highlighted the coalition between MADD, the PLCB, and other state and federal agencies involved with underage drinking, drunk driving, and other alcohol related issues.

Powerful lobbying groups, such as MADD or the NRA, possess the ability to quickly influence public policy. By highlighting a specific issue, lobbying groups can motivate the misinformed public, and then pressure Congress for a legislative response (Weitzer, 2005). Legislators, not wanting to look soft on crime or as opposing anything that addresses public safety, quickly react by drafting and passing legislation that may have little plausible chance of correcting the perceived problem. This situation, in turn, offers a potential answer to the second question posed above concerning why is Pennsylvania's zero-tolerance juvenile drunk driving law ineffective in controlling juvenile drunk driving and the corresponding fatality accidents.

Theoretically, deterrence theory suggests that increases in the certainty, proportional severity, or swiftness of receiving a sanction should prevent most people from offending. Research about underage drinking and juvenile drunk driving often fails to support, or finds only minimal support for these propositions (e.g., Corbett & Simon, 1992; Hilton, 1984; Hingson et al., 1987; Muller, 1989; Paternoster, 1989; Pogarsky, 2002; Ross et al., 1981; Tibbetts, 1997). Initially, these research results bring into question the empirical support for deterrence theory as it relates to underage drinking and juvenile drunk driving. In reality, it may not be a question of deterrence theory, but rather a question of how the law materialized.

Deterrence theory assumes a consensus approach to crime, in that any law reflects the beliefs and values of the majority of the people in the society (i.e., that law derives from societal beliefs and values, not vise versa). Thus, the legal sanctions proposed by the law are reinforced with social sanctions and social condemnation for transgressions against society should the law be violated. If laws are passed, which are not based on consensus, the offender can cautiously dismiss the social sanctions. Laws which are passed based on the interests of special groups, or moralistic crusaders, must rely primarily on legal sanctions to deter would-be offenders, since the majority of society may not concur that the act is criminal, or even deviant.

It does appear that the origins of underage drinking laws may be somewhat more readily explainable from the interactionist or social reaction rather than the consensus perspective; it could be that they are more the result of moralistic crusading, rather than to have bubbled up from a shared value system. In support of this assumption, the National Minimum Drinking Age Act of 1984 did not prohibit those under the age of 21 from drinking, it only directed that the states mandate the age of 21 for those who could purchase or publicly possess alcohol (Hanson, 2005). Seven states, to include Pennsylvania, and the District of Columbia passed legislation prohibiting anyone under the age of 21 from consuming alcohol. The other 43 states enacted legislation which restricted alcohol consumption for those under age 21 (23 states) or maintained a consumption age under 21, with restrictions on purchase and where alcohol consumption could occur (20 states).

Overall, 86% of the states did not comply with the intent of the federal mandate, but drafted legislation to evade increasing the legal drinking age, while sufficiently complying with the mandate to ensure federal highway funds. For example, in Ohio, a person 18 years old or older can consume alcohol (not purchase) in the presence of his/her parents, spouse (if the spouse is 21 years old or older), or legal guardian (Ohio Law, Sect. 4301.69). Further, Ohio legislation states that should the federal government repeal the Uniformed Drinking Age Act, Ohio's legal drinking age would immediately revert to 19 years of age.

With 86% of the states passing legislation to circumvent the federal drinking age mandate, along with the perceived lack of social condemnation for underage drinking, adults and juveniles become confused. The intent and usefulness of our current underage drinking policies come into question when a teen is permitted to legally consume alcohol in one location, but not another or with one group of individuals but not with another.

The decision to raise the legal drinking age to 21 and to lower the juvenile BAC level to establish drunk driving may be perceived as a form of mass punishment, in that all juveniles between the ages of 18 and 20 are being punished for what a few might do if permitted access to alcohol. The punishment is not being denied alcohol, but rather is the denial of their status as mature enough adults to make their own decisions about alcohol use; a decision that 43 states have determined is best not made by special interest groups acting through the federal government. If the origins of underage drinking laws are perceived by juveniles and adults to be more readily explainable as a social reaction, the threat of social sanctions would be severely diminished. The extent to which juveniles hold this perception and also the perceptions of adults about the severity of and appropriate reactions to juvenile alcohol use would seem to be important questions for future research.

Developmental. From a developmental perspective, juveniles are seeking adult status (Arnett, 2000, Moffitt, 1993). These "rights of passage" to adulthood include obtaining a driver's license at age 16, voting and decision making (not legally needing parental permission) at age 18, and finally alcohol consumption at age 21. For whatever reason, underage drinking is the last status offense identifying a young adult as a juvenile. The U.S. appears to send mixed signals to juveniles about when adult status is obtained. At age 18, we, as a society, appear to confer adult status on juveniles. At this age, an individual can legally, without parental consent: 1) leave home; 2) join the armed services; 3) vote; 4) get married; 5) make medical decisions; 6) purchase tobacco products; 7) enter in to legally binding contracts; 8) be tried only as an adult in a court of law; and, 9) receive the death penalty for the commission of certain criminal acts. Still, with all these new found responsibilities, an 18 year old is still perceived (by the government) as too irresponsible to make informed decisions about alcohol use, but even here, society sends these youths mixed signals.

As previously discussed, the National Minimum Drinking Age Act of 1984 did not prohibit those under the age of 21 from drinking, it only directed that the states mandate the age of 21 for those who could purchase or publicly possess alcohol (Hanson, 2005). Many states seem to send the message that their underage drinking laws originated from federal mandates, rather than to have bubbled up from a shared value system, thus sending mixed signals about alcohol use to 18 through 20 year olds. Further, our medical community tends to contradict the political position about abstention from alcohol use.

The National Institute on Alcohol Abuse and Alcoholism (NIAAA) reported that moderate alcohol consumption (1 – 3 drinks daily) places a person at less of a health risk than either abstaining from alcohol or abusing alcohol: "50 studies demonstrated an inverse association between light to moderate drinking and total morality under all scenarios" (Gunzerath, Faden, Zakhari, & Warren, 2004, p. 841). The report, which "now serves as the National Institutes of Health's formal position paper on the health risks and potential benefits of moderate alcohol use" (Gunzerath et al., p. 829) indicates that moderate alcohol use provides protection against coronary heart disease, reducing annually 80,000 deaths that would have occurred through alcohol abstention (Pearson & Terry, 1994). Further, the researchers noted that moderate alcohol use may reduce the risk of diabetes and metabolic syndrome, reduce the effects of aging, and may have no effects on cognitive functioning.

From a developmental perspective, it would appear that society is sending a mixed signal to juveniles about alcohol use. On one hand, it is socially acceptable (if age 21 or older, and in many states at a younger age in the presence of parents/guardians) and there are even some reports of medical benefits from moderate consumption; but on the other hand, the message is that those individuals between the ages of 18 and 20 are too irresponsible on their own to be entrusted not to abuse alcohol. As a means of preventing what might occur, legislation prohibits purchasing alcohol and limits use to certain situations for those under 21 years of age. It would seem to be a reasonable conclusion that these mixed signals about social acceptability of juvenile alcohol use, conference of adult status, and the health effects of moderate alcohol use need to be resolved before our juvenile alcohol policies can be fully effective.

Causation. A third plausible reason for the lack of empirical support for the deterrent approach to reduce juvenile traffic accident fatalities is that the majority of juvenile fatality accidents (65%) do not involve alcohol, and only about 2% involve a juvenile driver with a Blood Alcohol Concentration between .01 and .09 mg/ml (the population targeted for enforcement by the zero-tolerance juvenile drunk driving legislation) (FARS, 2003). The cause of most juvenile fatality accidents appears to be their lack of experience in safely operating a motor vehicle, which is compounded by alcohol use, but which also is compounded by excessive speed, weather conditions, darkness, the number of friends in the vehicle, the use of cell phones, driving too fast for road conditions, fatigue, etc. (e.g., IIHS, 2005; McMillan, 2005; NHTSA, 2003a; Simons-Morton, Hartos, Leaf, Preusser, 2005).

According to the National Safety Council (NSC), drivers age 16 to 20, only make-up about 6% of the nation's licensed drivers, but account for almost 20 % of all vehicle related fatality accidents. The NSC indicates that 25% of all vehicle accidents are the result of distractions, often caused by mobile electronic products (McMillan, 2005).

The Insurance Institute for Highway Safety (IIHS) reports that juveniles between the ages of 16 and 20 are three times more likely to be killed in a vehicle accident than in a homicide, and four times more likely to be in a traffic accident than drivers 21 years old and older (IIHS, 2005). The IIHS attributes the higher accident rate to immaturity (speeding, tailgating, impressing peers, not wearing safety belts), driving inexperience (distracted, over estimated driving ability, too fast for road and weather conditions), and the operation of older vehicles (less safety features and reliability). Although the NSC and IIHS both acknowledge that alcohol use is a contributing factor to vehicle accidents, especially if the driver's BAC exceeds .08, they also acknowledge more plausible causes other than alcohol use, which have not been deemed as criminal behavior (i.e., other juveniles in vehicle, cell phones, lack of adequate driver training).

By focusing on only one of the factors that enhance the possibility of an accident (alcohol use), we may be failing to address the more prominent sets of causal factors, which is juvenile driving skill and related driving behaviors. Further, by focusing on minor alcohol consumption, we are passing legislation which, according to available data, at best can only resolve 2% of juvenile motor-vehicle fatalities. Finally, most juvenile and adult alcohol-related fatality accidents occur when the vehicle operator has a BAC of .16 or higher (Fatality Analysis Reporting System, 2003). Reducing the BAC limit from .10 to .02 arguably will have only a minimal impact, if any, on those who already operate above the existing BAC limit for drunk driving. Balko (2005) equates this approach to "lowering the speed limit from 55 to 50 to catch motorists who zip along at 100 miles per hour" (p. 1).

Policy Alternatives

Since the early 1980s, the U.S. has aggressively attempted to control juvenile alcohol use through deterrence-based policies, such as increasing the legal drinking age and lowering the BAC level necessary to charge a juvenile with drunk driving. The literature is void of studies which empirically support this approach. To the contrary, the empirical evidence suggests that this approach is not only ineffective in deterring juvenile alcohol use, but increases the perception of a national juvenile alcohol problem by creating new categories for alcohol-related juvenile offending. Further, there is reasonable doubt about the level at which the general public supports this approach to controlling juvenile alcohol use, in that 43 of 50 states have drafted and passed legislation to circumvent alcohol-related federal mandates.

In developing policies to address underage drinking, and the associated juvenile drunk driving, objectives must be clearly identified. In other words, what are we, as a society, trying to gain by enacting legislation to restrict the use of alcohol? Although a common goal appears to be the prevention of alcohol abuse, to obtain this, current laws are focusing on eliminating alcohol use. By restricting alcohol use until the age of 21, the U.S. fails to educate juveniles about responsible, moderate drinking. The assumption is that at age 21, without any previous experience, individuals will be sufficiently mature to deal with alcohol.

If lowering juvenile alcohol related incidents, to include fatality accidents, is the goal, we must concede that our current approach is ineffective, especially when compared to those countries which have established a lower age for alcohol consumption (see for e.g., Jacobs, 1989; Richburg, 2004; Snortum, Hauge, & Berger, 1986). Thus, a more realistic approach might be education and moderation, starting at an earlier age and under parental management. A policy could be designed similar to the graduated programs for drivers' licensing, which would support alcohol use, but condemn alcohol abuse.

For example, at age 16, juveniles could consume alcohol in the presence of their parents. At age 18, juveniles could purchase (in certain quantities) and consume alcohol, having to depart from alcohol serving establishments at midnight. Finally, at 21, all alcohol restrictions would be removed. A national BAC limit for drunk driving could be established at .05, which supports the medical evaluation for acceptable alcohol use and would be supported by MADD. The foundation for such an approach can be found in the work of the influential learning theorist B.F. Skinner (1953):

> In asserting that "ignorance of the law is no excuse," the governmental agency leaves the actual conditioning of the individual to others. Parents and friends establish minor contingencies, which keep behavior within legal bounds, and the governmental function may also be actively supported by the ethical group and by religious and educational institutions (p. 339).

An education and moderation approach would take alcohol off of the pedestal on which it now currently resides. Further, by adhering to the 21st Amendment of the U.S. Constitution and permitting each of the states to establish their own drinking age and BAC level for drunk driving, state laws presumably would more directly reflect the will of the local citizenry, and violations of the law would carry not only legal sanctions, but also more social and personal sanctions. Laws that are supported by strong societal norms often are adhered to, regardless of the threat of legal sanctions (Tittle & Logan, 1973).

Under current policy, we arguably are diluting the social and personal sanctions associated with drunk driving by charging juveniles with this offense, when state legislatures, parents, and many others in society do not agree with the law's definition of impairment. For example, in the early 1960s adultery was illegal and most people did not speak openly about alternative life styles or divorce. Today, these topics have lost much of their social stigmatism as occurrences have become more common place.

As a society, we risk losing the currently high, and necessary, social stigmatism associated with drunk driving as we charge more drivers, especially juvenile drivers, with offenses that fail to meet society's standards for that offense. Through personal and vicarious experiences more people (especially the next generation of adults) will know individuals who have been cited for drunk driving, but were neither drunk nor impaired, except by a legal definition. As more juveniles (and plausibly more adults if MADD can advance legislation for an adult BAC limit of .05 mg/ml) are arrested for alcohol use and drunk driving with a BAC below .08 mg/ml, the nation runs the risk of socially minimizing the charge of drunk driving with a BAC over .08 mg/ml.

A second policy recommendation could be to look to the European countries to identify how they have legislated juvenile alcohol use. If their policies are deemed effective, they could be adopted. It would be necessary to adopt the program in its entirety and not select only the restrictive components such as lowering the BAC to constitute drunk driving for adults to .05 mg/ml, which has been suggested by MADD. European countries increase driver licensing standards, while permitting juveniles to consume alcohol at an early age, thus placing parental and not state responsibility for juvenile alcohol use (Hanson, 2005). This model relates to Skinner's (1953) observation that individuals actually come to abide by a code not through governmental agencies, but through parents and friends who keep behavior within legal bounds.

A third policy option would be to continue with the deterrence approach, which in its current form appears to lack the perceived social and personal sanctions necessary to be an effective deterrent for many juveniles. Empirical support suggests that if the goal of restricting juvenile alcohol use is truly to save lives, this approach would remain ineffective without social support, a unanimous theme also identified in the law enforcement interviews. To gain social support, a majority of society must be convinced that underage drinking causes "real" health and physical risks. Currently, the scientific evidence does not exist that shows more than a correlation between juvenile alcohol use and future health risks and/or criminal behavior. What does exist in society are adults who have personal and vicarious experience with juvenile alcohol use, which often counters the medical and academic claims about the causal link between juvenile alcohol use and future health/physical/criminal risks.

However, if restricting adult and juvenile alcohol use is only loosely related to health and safety reasons, as part of a larger moralistic campaign, deterrence-based policies must be applied, thus using the Criminal Justice System as the enforcement arm against a society which has not accepted the crusade. Further, any policy recommendation that would suggest less restrictive alternatives for juvenile and adult alcohol use, even if proven effective in reducing alcohol related fatalities and incidents, would not be an acceptable alternative if prohibition is the goal.

In summary, multiple studies have identified that our current deterrence-based policy approach to preventing juvenile alcohol use and juvenile alcohol-related injuries is not working. This study supplies additional support that a zero-tolerance approach, while significantly increasing juvenile drunk driving arrest rates, also appears ineffective in lowering juvenile alcohol-related traffic fatalities.

It is suggested here, that the lack of current policy effectiveness is likely a combination of the three potential causes (social consensus, developmental, and causation). Although each of the potential causes offers a different perspective as to why deterrence based policies and laws seem to fail to deter infrequent behaviors such as juvenile DUI, as noted above, their policy implications are compatible and the combination of which may in fact constitute a more comprehensive and workable approach.

Current juvenile alcohol use policies appear to lack social and personal sanctions, which are key components to policy adherence and deterrence theory (consensus). The social sanctions attached to current policy appear to be more about law adherence to avoid legal entanglements, than they are about truly believing juveniles should not be permitted to consume alcohol. Unless the general public can be convinced of the latter, that juveniles under the age of 21 should not consume alcohol for reasons other than the purely legal, social support will remain minimal and policy violations will continue. As policy violations continue, additional deterrence legislation will be mandated, creating new crimes, just as the failure of the uniformed drinking age legislation resulted in lower juvenile BAC limits for establishing drunk driving. The perception of increased offending, based on new crimes, will give the appearance that the problem has worsened, suggesting the need for more deterrence-based legislation.

The key to a comprehensive juvenile alcohol use policy would be one that promotes and permits responsible alcohol use, while minimizing alcohol abuse. Alternative policy options were suggested to break this legislative cycle. Although these options may appear politically incorrect to some legislatures and special interest groups, they offer an alternative method in attempting to reduce juvenile alcohol related fatalities by deemphasizing alcohol use and stressing parental and personal responsibility and accountability.

Appendix A

Types of Effects

In reporting treatment effects for time series designs, researchers should discuss whether the treatment caused a change in the slope and/or trend of the data; whether the change, if any, was gradual or abrupt (onset); whether the change was permanent or temporary (duration); and finally, was the change immediate or delayed (immediacy) (McDowall et al., 1980; Shadish et al., 2002). Figure A1 displays time series data with an intervention or treatment at observation #49. The data remains uninterrupted by the treatment, with no change in slope, trend, onset, duration, or immediacy.

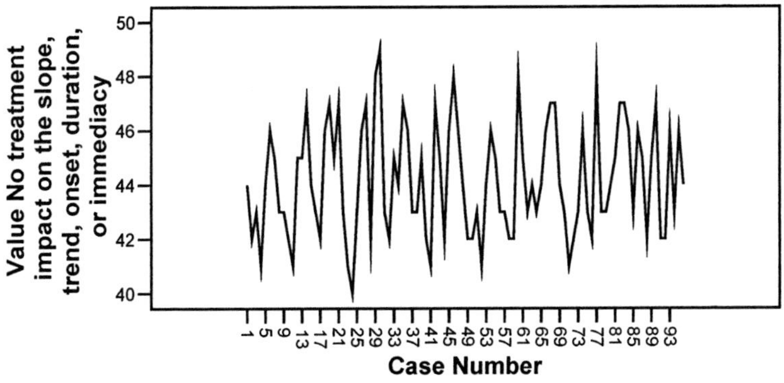

Figure A1. No treatment impact.

Figure A2 displays an abrupt, permanent, and immediate impact on the slope at the treatment point (observation #49).

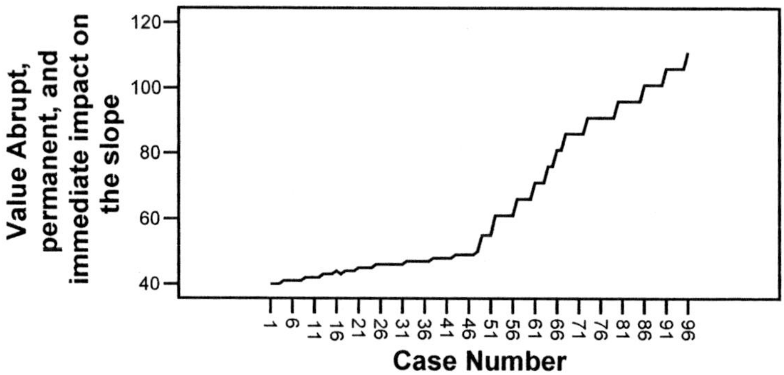

Figure A2. Abrupt, permanent, and immediate impact.

Figure A3 displays an abrupt, permanent, and immediate change in the level of the data at the intervention or treatment point (observation #49). The change in the level or intercept causes the post-treatment slope to have a different y-intercept than the pre-treatment slope even though the two slopes are virtually identical.

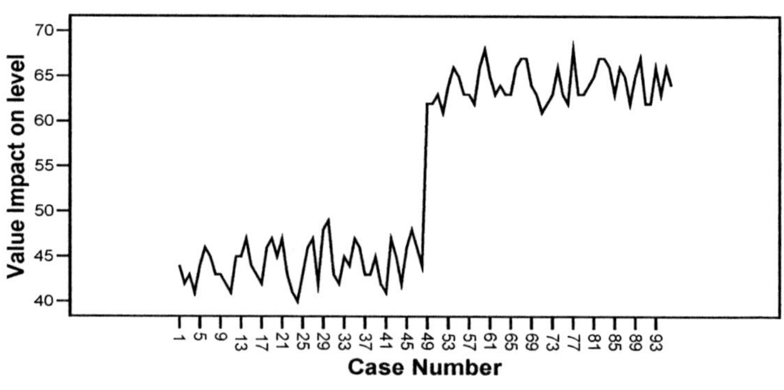

Figure A3. Abrupt, permanent, and immediate impact.

Figure A4 displays a gradual, permanent, but delayed impact on the level. Although the treatment was introduced at observation #49, the effect appeared to be delayed until observation #56, almost an eight-month period. After displaying a gradual increase to a new level, the observations stabilize and indicate a permanent effect.

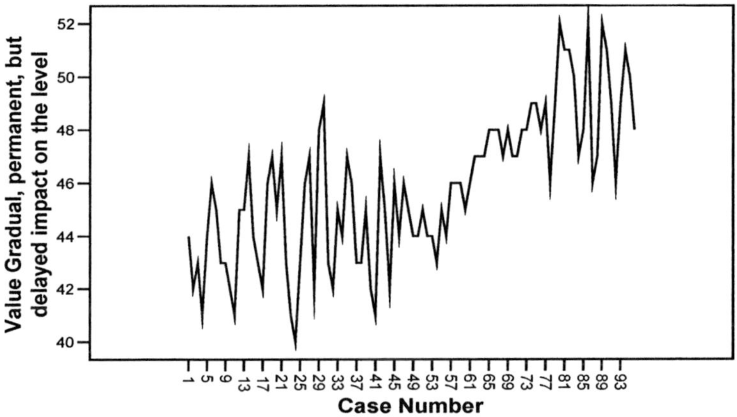

Figure A4. Gradual, permanent, but delayed impact on the level.

The fifth impact example is that of an abrupt, immediate, but temporary impact on the level, with a gradual return to pre-treatment levels. This pattern is the most prevalent effect identified in the literature surrounding the impact of drinking and driving legislation, and is also the predictive model for pre- and post-treatment observations of Pennsylvania's zero-tolerance juvenile drunk driving legislation. Based on previous literature, immediately after the treatment is introduced, juvenile drunk driving arrest rates should increase based on the lower standards for charging juvenile drunk drivers, aggressive enforcement of the new law, and the lack of personal and vicarious experience about the certainty of enforcement of the new law. It is anticipated, again based on past literature about implementation of drunk driving laws, that the increase in arrest rates will eventually peak and start a gradual decline to pre-treatment levels. The arrest rates should peak between 4 and 6 months, with the gradual return to pre-intervention levels occurring within 12 to 24 months after the law was enacted.

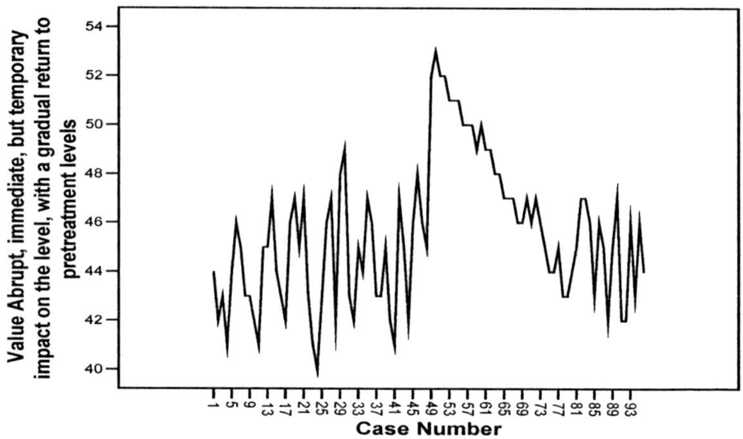

Figure A5. Abrupt, immediate, but temporary impact on the level, with a gradual return to pre-treatment levels.

Figure A6 indicates the impact of the treatment based on a simplistic view of deterrence theory where only certainty, severity and swiftness are considered. The law, being well publicized by state and local media and law enforcement agencies prior to implementation has an immediate, abrupt, and permanent effect on both the level and slope, causing observations of post-treatment juvenile drunk driving arrest rates to drop significantly. As certainty and severity of punishment is learned through personal and vicarious experiences, rational thinking juveniles refrain from committing the offense of drunk driving. The pain or cost associated with the increased certainty of getting caught and the increased severity of potential sanctions would negate the pleasure or benefits associated with drinking and driving.

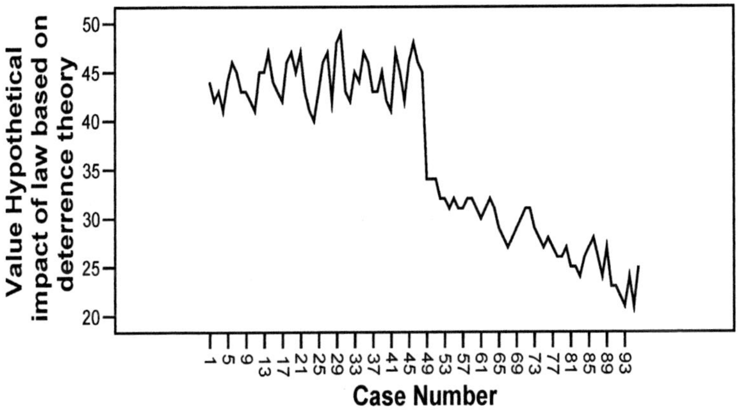

Figure A6. Hypothetical impact of law based on deterrence theory.

The results displayed in Figure A6 were those anticipated using a simplistic view of deterrence theory. The results displayed in Figure A7 indicate what Beccaria (1764/1986) would term creating crime. Figure A7 offers a more realistic view of how the actual data might appear based on the underlying assumptions of deterrence theory. Beccaria suggests that laws cannot be used to regulate morality, virtues and vices. Additionally, laws must be based on consensus and not conflict or interactionism.

Base on these unarticulated assumptions it would be hypothesized that the impact of the law was a significant increase in level of arrest, which was immediate, abrupt, and permanent. The enactment of the law has failed to deter juvenile drivers from operating motor vehicles, while at lower BAC levels, causing more arrests due to the lower BAC standards established to constitute drunk driving. Further, the law has failed to impact juvenile fatality motor vehicle accident rates caused by juvenile drunk drivers, since data suggest that higher blood alcohol levels are associated with fatality accidents.

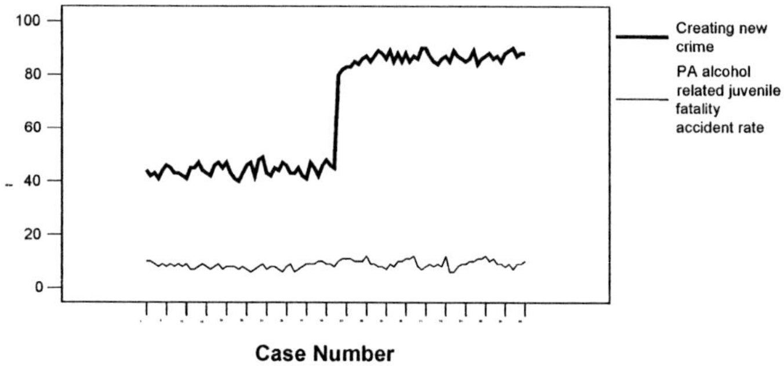

Figure A7. Creating new crime.

Appendix B

Newspaper Media Search

Hypothetically, pre-treatment media coverage about the law would increase individual awareness and would restrict offending. A media effect, if present, could affect the location of the y-intercept at the time the law was enforceable and could impact the trend in both the pre- and post-treatment observations immediately surrounding the treatment area.

A search was conducted in 32 newspapers published in Pennsylvania and press releases from the Pennsylvania Liquor Control Board (PLCB). The search focused on any newspaper article or PLCB press release printed between August 1995 and September 2005 that related to "zero-tolerance" "underage drinking" or "fatality accidents." The search resulted in 14 newspaper articles being identified as related to the search criteria.

Blairsville Dispatch (PA)
Bucks County Courier Times (Levittown, PA)
Butler Eagle (PA)
Centre Daily Times (State College, PA)
Citizen's Voice, The & Sunday Voice (Wilkes-Barre, PA)
Daily Courier (Connellsville, PA)

Daily News, The (Lebanon, PA)
Daily Review, The & Sunday Review (Towanda, PA)
Electric City (Scranton, PA)
Erie Times-News (PA)
Evening Sun, The (Hanover, PA)
Intelligencer, The (Doylestown, PA)
Lancaster Newspapers Inc. (PA)
Leader Times (Kittanning, PA)
Morning Call, The (Allentown, PA)
New Castle News (PA)
News-Item, The (Shamokin, PA)
Observer-Reporter (Washington, PA)
Philadelphia Daily News (PA)
Philadelphia Inquirer, The (PA)
Pittsburgh Post-Gazette (PA)
Pittsburgh Tribune-Review (PA)
Pottsville Republican, The & Evening Herald (PA)
Public Opinion (Chambersburg, PA)
Times Leader, The (Wilkes-Barre, PA)
Times-Tribune, The (Scranton, PA)
Tribune-Review (Greensburg, PA)
Valley Advantage, The (Olyphant, PA)
Valley Independent, The (Monessen, PA)
Valley News Dispatch (New Kensington, PA)
York Daily Record/York Sunday News (PA)
York Dispatch, The (PA)

Appendix C

Fatality Analysis Reporting System (FARS) Data and Models

Figure C1 – Figure C4 were extracted from Pennsylvania Department of Transportation data and data from the NHTSA's FAR System. Figure C1 suggests that in the early 1990s, Pennsylvania's alcohol related fatality accident rates were higher than those not involving alcohol. The trend changed around 1994.

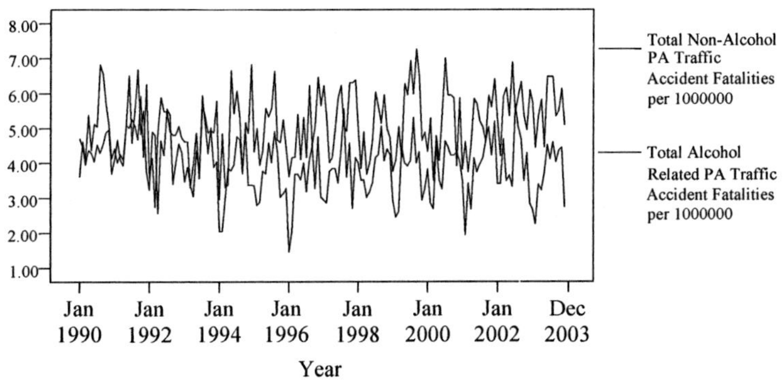

Figure C1.
Pennsylvania vehicle related fatalities per 1,000,000 licensed Pennsylvania drivers (1990 – 2003).

Figure C2 displays Pennsylvania's fatality rates for drivers under the age of 21with and without alcohol involvement. Similar to Figure C1, juvenile alcohol related fatalities were comparable to non-alcohol related fatalities until approximately 1994. What is questionable is the severity of the problem with alcohol related juvenile driver fatalities. Pennsylvania's Department of Transportation indicated that there are approximately 500, 000 drivers in the state under the age of 21; Thus, the deaths caused by this group, on average, was less than five per month. Although any death that is avoidable is tragic, the targeting of this particular group appears questionable when additional measures were not implemented by the state in an attempt to reduce the higher rate of fatality accidents by juveniles who were not using alcohol. The data suggest the problem is not as much alcohol use as overall driving ability and the need for early and more comprehensive driver training programs and plausibly stricter licensing requirements.

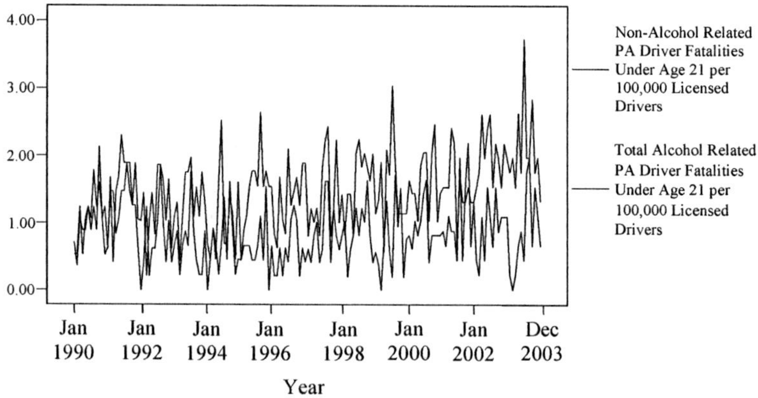

Figure C2.
Pennsylvania juvenile drivers killed in vehicle accidents (1990 – 2003).

Figure C3 displays a comparison of non-alcohol related fatality accidents with alcohol related fatality accidents for Pennsylvania adult drivers. Having followed the drunk driving literature in Pennsylvania since the early 1980s, one plausible interpretation of the data is that in the early 1990s Pennsylvania had a severe problem with drinking and driving fatalities. As the data indicate, in many months prior to 1994, the alcohol related fatality numbers where greater than the non-alcohol related fatality numbers.

In 1994 and 1995, the state enacted legislation to increase the sanctions for drunk driving and also started a media campaign using billboards to indicate "Drunk Driving – You can't afford it" or a billboard with the picture of a trooper with the caption "My job is to catch drunk drivers." The data suggests that the media campaign and threat of severe sanctions worked as a deterrent throughout the 1990's. Starting in about 2001, the fear of sanctions for whatever reason dissipated, as non-alcohol related fatalities remained relatively constant, while those involving alcohol increased.

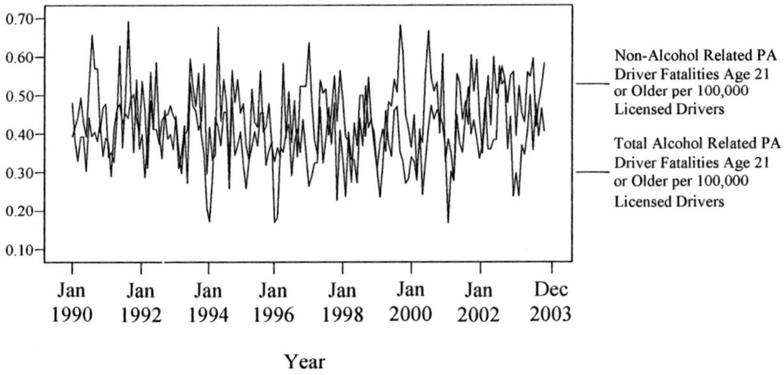

Figure C3.
Pennsylvania adult drivers killed in vehicle accidents (1990 – 2003).

Figure C4is presented to indicate why the lowering of the BAC level from .10 to .02 in an attempt to reduce alcohol related juvenile fatality traffic accidents was ineffective legislation at least in Pennsylvania. As indicated, those drivers with a BAC between .01 and .09 are not those who are causing the fatality accidents. FARS data suggests that the average BAC for a drunk driver involved in a fatality accident is .16. Pennsylvania data supports the FARS data in that those with higher BAC levels also are those more likely to be involved in a fatality accident.

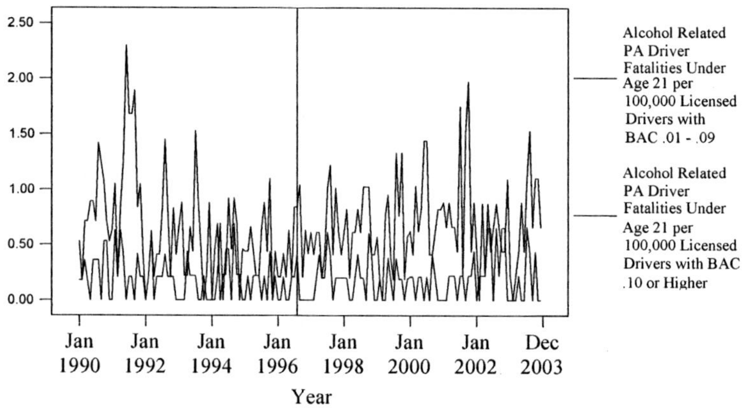

Figure C4.
Pennsylvania intoxicated juvenile drivers killed in vehicle accidents (1990 – 2003).

References

Akers, R. L. (2000). *Criminological theories: Introduction, evaluation, and application (3rd Ed.).* Los Angeles: Roxbury Publishing Company.

Archambeault, W. G. (1979). *Evaluating the utility of the deterrent residual in predicting deterrent outcomes in a self-report study: A comparative analysis of the Beccarian and Benthamite models of deterrence theory.* Ann Arbor, MI: University Microfilms International.

Arnett, J. J. (2000, May). Emerging adulthood: A theory of development from the late teens through the twenties. *American Psychologist, 55,* 469 – 480.

Balko, R. (2005, October 30). Forum: Lower DUI threshold more dangerous? http://www.cato.org/pub_display.php?pub_id=5167

Beccaria, C. (1986). *On crimes and punishments.* (D. Young, Trans.) Indianapolis, IN: Hackett Publishing Company. (Original work published 1764).

Bishop, D. M. (1982). *Deterrence and social control: A longitudinal study of the effects of sanctioning and social bonding on the prevention of delinquency.* Ann Arbor, MI: University Microfilms International.

Britt, C. L., Kleck, G., & Bordua, D. J. (1996). A reassessment of the D.C. gun law: Some cautionary notes on the use of interrupted time series designs for policy impact assessments. *Law & Society Review, 30,* 361 – 380.

Brown, D. W. (1978). Arrest rates and crime rates: When does a tipping effect occur? *Social Forces, 57,* 671 – 682.

Chermack, S. T. & Giancola, P. R. (1997). The relationship between alcohol and aggression: An integrated bio-psychosocial conceptualization. *Clinical Psychology Review, 17,* 621 – 649.

Cohn, L. D., MacFarlane, S., Yanez, C., & Imai, W. K. (1995). Risk perception: Between adolescents and adults. *Health Psychology, 14,* 217 – 222.

Corbett, C. & Simon, F. (1992). Decisions to break or adhere to the rules of the road, viewed from the rational choice perspective. *British Journal of Criminology, 32,* 537 – 549.

Creswell, J. W. (1994). *Research design: Qualitative and quantitative approaches.* Thousand Oaks, CA: Sage Publications.

Dishion, T. J., Andrews, D. W., & Crosby, L. (1995). Antisocial boys and their friends in early adolescence: Relationship characteristics, quality, and interactional processes. *Child Development, 66,* 139 – 151.

Donohew, R. L., Hoyle, R. H., Clayton, R. R., Skinner, W. F., Colon, S. E., & Rice, R. E. (1999). Sensation seeking and drug use by adolescents and their friends: Models for marijuana and alcohol. *Journal of Studies on Alcohol, 60,* 622 – 631.

Donovan, J. E. (1993). Young adult drinking-driving: Behavioral and psychosocial correlates. *Journal of Studies on Alcohol, 54,* 600 – 613.

Dunn, W. N. (1994). *Public policy analysis: An introduction (2nd Ed.).* Englewood Cliffs: NJ. Prentice Hall. Erickson, M. L., Gibbs, J. P., & Jensen, G. F. (1977). The deterrence doctrine and the perceived certainty of legal punishments. *American Sociological Review, 42,* 305 – 317.

Esterberg, K. G. (2002). *Qualitative methods in social research.* Boston, MA: McGraw-Hill Companies.

Evans, W. N., Neville, D. & Graham, J. D. (1991). General deterrence of drunk driving: Evaluation of recent American policies. *Risk Analysis, 11,* 279 – 289.

Exum, M. L. (2002). The application and robustness of the rational choice perspective in the study of intoxicated and angry intentions to aggress. *Criminology, 40,* 933 – 966.

Fatality Analysis Reporting System (FARS). (2003). National Highway Transportation Safety Administration: National Center for Statistics and Analysis. http://www-fars.nhtsa.dot.gov.

Figlio, D. N. (1995). The effect of drinking age laws and alcohol-related crashes: Time-Series evidence from Wisconsin. *Journal of Policy Analysis and Management, 14,* 555 – 556.

Gerrard, M., Gibbons, F. X., Benthin, A. C., & Hessling, R. M. (1996). A longitudinal study of the reciprocal nature of risk behaviors and cognitions in adolescents: What you do shapes what you think, and vice versa. *Health Psychology, 15,* 344 – 354.

Gibbs, J. P. (1975). *Crime, punishment, and deterrence.* New York: Elsevier.

Gottfredson, M. R. & Hirschi, T. (1990). *A general theory of crime*. Stanford, CA: Stanford University Press.

Grasmick, H. G. & Bursik, R. J., Jr. (1990). Conscience, significant others, and rational choice: Extending the deterrence model. *Law & Society Review, 24,* 837 – 861.

Gunzerath, L., Faden, V., Zakhari, S., & Warren, K. (2004). National Institute on Alcohol Abuse and Alcoholism report on moderate drinking. *Alcoholism: Clinical and Experimental Research, 28,* 829 – 847.

Hagan, J. (Ed.) (1982). *Deterrence reconsidered: Methodological innovations.* Beverly Hills, CA: Sage Publications.

Hamilton, W. (2000). Lessons learned along the way: Starting a non-profit organization. http://www.madd.org/aboutus/0,1056,1122,00.html

Hamilton, W. J. (2004). Mothers against drunk driving: Annual Report 2003 - 2004. http://www.madd.org/docs/2004-annual-noLetter.pdf

Hanson, D. J. (2005). Alcohol: Problems and solutions. http://www2.potsdam.edu/hansondj/LegalDrinkingAge.html

Hedlund, J. H., Ulmer, R. G., & Preusser, D. F. (2001). Determine why there are fewer young alcohol-impaired drivers. Preusser Research Group, Inc. http://www.nhtsa.dot.gov/people/injury/research/FewerYoungDrivers/iv__what_caused.htm

Hilton, M. (1984). The impact of recent changes in California drinking-driving laws on fatal accident levels during the first post-intervention year: An interrupted time series analysis. *Law and Society Review, 18,* 605 – 627.

Hingson, R. (1993). Prevention of alcohol-impaired driving. *Alcohol Health and Research World, 17,* 28 – 34.

Hingson, R., Heeren, T., Kovenock, D., Mangione, T., Meyers, A., Morelock, S., Lederman, R., & Scotch, N. (1987). Effects of Maine's 1981 and Massachusetts' 1982 driving-under-the-influence legislation. *American Journal of Public Health, 77,* 593 – 597.

Hingson, R. & Winter, M. (2003, December). Epidemiology and consequences of drinking and driving. *National Institute on Alcohol Abuse.* www.niaaa.nih.gov/publications/arh27-1/63-78.htm

IIHS (2005). Insurance Institute for Highway Safety fatality facts 2004: Teenagers. http://www.iihs.org/research/fatality_facts/pdfs/teenagers.pdf

Jacobs, J. B. (1989). *Drunk driving: An American dilemma.* Chicago: University of Chicago Press.

Johnson, A. (1994, February 04). Drinking may mean trouble: Tougher new law. *The Columbus Dispatch (Ohio),* pp. 1B.

Johnson, J. L. & Saint Germain, M. A. (2005). Officer down: Implications of three strikes for public safety. *Criminal Justice Policy Review, 16,* 443 – 460.

Johnston, L. D., O'Malley, P. M., Bachman, J. G., & Schulenberg, J. E. (2004). *Monitoring the future and national results on adolescent drug use: Overview of key findings 2003. (NIH Publications No: 04-5506).* Bethesda, MD: National Institute on Drug Abuse.

Katz, C. M., Webb, V. J., & Schaefer, D. R. (2001). An assessment of the impact of quality-of-life policing on crime and disorder. *Justice Quarterly, 18,* 825 – 876.

Krimmel, J. T., & Mele, M. (1998). Investigating stolen vehicle dumpsites: An interrupted time series quasi-experiment. *Policing, 21,* 479 – 488.

Lanza-Kaduce, L. (1988). Perceptual deterrence and drinking and driving among college students. *Criminology, 26,* 321 – 341.

Legge, J. S., Jr. & Park, J. (1994). Policies to reduce alcohol-impaired driving: Evaluating elements of deterrence. *Social Science Quarterly, 75.* 594 – 606.

Lempert, R. (1966). Strategies of research design in the legal impact study: The control of plausible rival hypotheses. *Law and Society Review, 1,* 111 – 132.

Levy, M. M. (2002). *U.S. Department of Transportation 2001 National Survey of Drinking and Driving, V. 1: Summary report.* http://www.nhtsa.html

Lewis-Beck, M. S. (1980). *Applied Regression: An Introduction.* Thousand Oaks, CA: Sage Publications Inc.

Lord, J. (2000, Spring). Really MADD: Looking back at 20 years. *Driven Magazine* http://www.madd.org/news.html

Maier, P. (1998). *The Declaration of Independence and the Constitution of the United States.* New York: Bantam Books.

Marks, G., Graham, J. W., & Hansen, W. B. (1992). Social projection and social conformity in adolescent alcohol use: A longitudinal analysis. *Personality and Social Psychology Bulletin, 18,* 96 – 101.

McDowall, D., McCleary, R., Meidinger, E. E., & Hay, R. A., Jr. (1980). *Interrupted Time Series Analysis.* Thousand Oaks, CA: Sage Publications Inc.

McGeveran, W. A., Jr. (2004). *The world almanac and book of facts 2004.* New York: World Almanac Books.

McLaughlin, P. (1985). Police management of public drunkenness in Scotland. *British Journal of Criminology, 25,* 344 – 361.

McMillan, A. C. (2005). National Safety Council 2005 annual report. http://www.nsc.org/public/annual_report_05.pdf

Moffitt, T. E. (1993). Adolescence-limited and life-course-persistent anti-social behavior: A developmental taxonomy. *Psychological Review, 100,* 674 – 704.

Mohr, L. B. (1988). *Impact analysis for program evaluation.* Pacific Grove, CA: Brooks/Cole Publishing Company.

Moody, C. E. & Marvell, T. B. (1996). The uncertain timing innovations in time series: Minnesota sentencing guidelines and jail sentences – a comment. *Criminology, 34,* 257 – 267.

Mosher, C. J., Miethe, T. D., & Phillips, D. M. (2002). *The mismeasure of crime.* Thousand Oaks, CA: Sage Publications.

Muller, A. (1989). Business recession, alcohol consumption, drinking and driving laws: Impact on Oklahoma motor vehicle fatalities and fatal crashes. *American Journal of Public Health, 79,* 1366 – 1370.

Nagin, D. S., & Paternoster, R. (1993). Enduring the differences and rational choice theories of crime. *Law and Society Review, 27.* 467 – 496.

Nagin, D. S. & Pogarsky, G. (2001). Integrating celerity, impulsivity, and extralegal sanction threats into a model of general deterrence theory and evidence. *Criminology, 39.* 865 – 892.

National Highway Transportation Safety Administration (2003a). *Traffic safety facts 2002.* National Center for Statistics and Analysis. http://www-nrd.nhtsa.dot.gov/pdf/nrd-30/NCSA/TSFAnn/TSF2002Final.pdf

National Highway Transportation Safety Administration (2003b). *Traffic safety facts 2002 (alcohol).* National Center for Statistics and Analysis. http://www.nhtsa.html.

Nejman, J. (2002, December 11). Opting to drink young affects other decisions. *The York Daily Record,* http:www.wellspan.org/Frontpage/ydr12112002.htm.

Nelson, C. R. (1973). *Applied time series analysis for managerial forecasting.* San Francisco, CA: Holden-Day Inc.

Olivero, M. J., Hansen, R., & Clark, A. M. (1993). An assessment of police implementation of the Texas public intoxication law in small cities: What is dangerous to self or others? *American Journal of Police, 12, (4),* 127 – 145.

Ostrom, C. W., Jr. (1990). *Time Series Analysis: Regression Techniques (2nd Ed).* Thousand Oaks, CA: Sage Publications Inc.

Paternoster, R. (1989). Absolute and restrictive deterrence in a panel of youth: Explaining the onset, persistence/desistance, and frequency of delinquent offending. *Social Problems, 36,* 289 – 309.

Paternoster, R. (1987). The deterrent effect of the perceived certainty and severity of punishment: A review of the evidence and issues. *Justice Quarterly, 4,* 173 – 217.

Paternoster, R. & Bachman, R. (2001). *Explaining criminals and crime.* Los Angeles, CA: Roxbury Publishing Company.

PCCD. (2004). 2003 PA youth survey. *PA Commission on Crime and Delinquency.* http//www.pccd.state.pa.us/pccd/stats/payouth survey/2003_pa_youth_survey_report.pdf

Pearson, T. A., & Terry, P. (1994). What to advise patients about drinking alcohol: The clinician's conundrum. *The Journal of the American Medical Association, 272,* 967-968.

Perkins, H. , Meilman, P. , Leichliter, J. S., Cashin, J., & Presley, C. A. (1999). Misperceptions of the norms for the frequency of alcohol and other drug use on college campuses. *Journal of American College Health, 47,* 253 – 259.

Piliavin, I., Thornton, C., Gartner, R., & Matsueda, R. L. (1986). Crime, deterrence, and rational choice. *American Sociological Review, 51,* 101 – 119.

Piquero, A. & Paternoster, R. (1998). An application of Stafford and Warr's reconceptualization of deterrence to drinking and driving. *Journal of Research in Crime and Delinquency, 35,* 3 – 39.

Piquero, A. & Rengert, G. F. (1999). Studying deterrence with active residential burglars. *Justice Quarterly, 16,* 451 – 471.

Pogarsky, G. & Piquero, A. R. (2003). Can punishment encourage offending? Investigating the "resetting" effect. *Journal of Research in Crime and Delinquency, 40,* 95 – 120.

Pogarsky, G. (2002). Identifying "deterrable" offenders: Implications for research on deterrence. *Justice Quarterly, 19,* 431 – 452.

Reynolds, K. M., Seydlitz, R., & Jenkins, P. (2000). Do juvenile curfew laws work? A time-series analysis of the New Orleans law. *Justice Quarterly, 17,* 205 – 229.

Richburg, K. B. (2004, December 30). European laws place emphasis on the driving, not the drinking. The Washington Post, pp. A12.

Ross, H. L. (1982). Interrupted time series studies of deterrence of drinking and driving In J. Hagan (Ed.) *Deterrence reconsidered: Methodological innovations* (pp. 71 – 97). Beverly Hills, CA: Sage Publications.

(1985). Deterring drunk driving: An analysis of current efforts. *Journal of Studies on Alcohol, 10,* 122 – 128.

Ross, H. L., McCleary, R., & Epperlein, T. (1981). Deterrence of drinking and driving in France: An evaluation of the law of July 12, 1978. *Law and Society Review, 16,* 345 – 373.

Saltzman, L., Paternoster, R., Waldo, G. P., & Chiricos, T. G. (1982). Deterrent and experiential effects: The problem of casual order in perceptual deterrence research. *Journal of Research in Crime and Delinquency, 19,* 172 – 189.

Scheider, M. C. (2001). Deterrence and the base rate fallacy: An examination of perceived certainty. *Justice Quarterly, 18,* 63 – 86.

Shadish, W. R., Cook, T. D., & Campbell, D. T. (2002). *Experimental and quasi-experimental designs for generalized causal inference.* New York: Houghton Mifflin Company.

Sherman L. W. & Weisburd, D. (1995). General deterrence effects of police patrol in crime "Hot Spots": A randomized, controlled trial. *Justice Quarterly, 12,* 625 –648.

Shope, J. T. & Bingham, C. R. (2002). Drinking-Driving as a component of problem driving and problem behavior in young adults. *Journal of Studies in Alcohol, 63,* 24 – 33.

Shore, E. R. & Maguin, E. (1988). Deterrence of drinking-driving: The effects of changes in Kansas driving under the influence law. *Evaluation and Program Planning - Special Issue: Alcohol and Traffic Safety, 11,* 245 – 254.

Simons-Morton, B. G., Hartos, J. L., Leaf, W. A., Preusser, D. F. (2005, March). Persistence of effects of the Checkpoints Program on parental restrictions of teen driving privileges. *American Journal of Public Health, 95,* 447 - 452.

Skinner, B. F. (1953). *Science and human behavior.* New York: The Free Press.

Snortum, J., Hauge, R., & Berger, D. (1986). Deterring alcohol impaired driving: A comparative analysis of compliance in Norway and the United States. *Justice Quarterly, 3,* 139 – 165.

Stafford, M. & Warr, M. (1993). A reconceptualization of general and specific deterrence. *Journal of Research in Crime and Delinquency, 30,* 123 – 135.

Swartzwelder, S. (1998, Fall). Brain 101. *Driven Magazine.* http://www.madd.org/stats/0,1056,1744,00.html

Tibbetts, S. G. (1997). Shame and rational choice in offending decisions. *Criminal Justice and Behavior, 24.* 234 – 255.

Tittle, C. R. & Logan, C. H. (1973). Sanctions and deviance: Evidence and remaining questions. *Law and Society Review, 7,* 371 – 392.

Tittle, C. R. & Rowe, A. R. (1974). Certainty of arrest and crime rates: A further test of the deterrence hypothesis. *Social Forces, 52,* 455 – 462.

Ward, D. A. & Tittle, Charles R. (1993). Deterrence or labeling: The effects of informal sanctions. *Deviant Behavior: An Interdisciplinary Journal, 14,* 43 – 64.

Weitzer, R. (2005, September/October). The growing moral panic over prostitution and sex trafficking. *The Criminologist,* 30, 1 – 5.

West, S. G., Hepworth, J. T., McCall, M. A., & Reich, J. W. (1989). An evaluation of Arizona's July 1982 Drunk Driving Law: Effects on the city of Phoenix. *Journal of Applied Social Psychology, 19,* 1212 – 1237.

Williams, F. P. III & McShane, M. D. (2004). Youth, drugs, and delinquency. In P. J. Benekos & A. V. Merlo (eds.), *Controversies in juvenile justice and delinquency* (pp. 69-88). Cincinnati, OH: Anderson Publishing/LexisNexis.

Williams, K. R. & Gibbs, J. P. (1981), Deterrence and knowledge of statutory penalties. *The Sociological Quarterly, 22,* 591 – 606.

Yu, J. (1994). Punishment celerity and severity: Testing a specific deterrence model on drunk driving recidivism. *Journal of Criminal Justice, 22.* 355 – 366.

Yu, J., & Liska, A. E. (1993). The certainty of punishment: A reference group effect and its functional form. *Criminology, 31,* 447 – 464.

Zimring, F. E. & Hawkins, G. J. (1973). *Deterrence: The legal threat of crime control.* Chicago: University of Chicago Press.

Zimring, F. E. & Hawkins, G. J. (1968). Deterrence and marginal groups. *Journal of Research in Crime and Delinquency, 2,* 100 –114.

Index